The Original Wisdom

of the

DAO DE JING

A New Translation and Commentary

by

P. J. LASKA

THE ORIGINAL WISDOM OF THE DAO DE JING:
A New Translation and Commentary

An ECCS Book published in paperback, 2012

ECCS Books
392 W. Rio Altar
Green Valley, AZ 85614

ISBN: 13: 978-06155110118
ISBN: 10: 0615510116

COVER IMAGE: Chen Hongshou (Chinese 1598-1652), *Paintings after Ancient Masters: Lao-Tzu Riding an Ox*; Album leaf, ink and color on silk, 24.3 x 22.6 cm, used with permission of The Cleveland Museum of Art, John L Severance Fund, 1979.27.1.2

Printed in the Unites States of America

The Way of Heaven
reduces excess
and supplements deficiency.
The Way of Men is different.
It takes from deficiency
to supplement excess.
--DDJ 77

CONTENTS

INTRODUCTION

The *Dao De Jing* is a classic of ancient Chinese philosophy and one of the great wisdom texts of world literature. Its origin is obscure but the recent discovery of "bamboo slips," containing partial texts of the *Dao De Jing* (referred in its early form as the *Laozi*) dating from the middle 4th century BCE, has provided new evidence that its composition most likely belongs to the early "Warring States" period (475-222 BCE).[1] The book has come down to us in the form given to it by the scholarly editors of the Han Dynasty (206 BCE-220 CE). In this form it is a collection of 81 "verses" assembled into two sections, titled "Dao" (37 verses) and "De" (44 verses). In ancient China it was thought to be the work of Laozi, chief archivist of the Zhou court, who may or may not have been a real historical personage. The name Laozi translates as "old master." *Dao De Jing* literally means "Way Attainment Classic," although the word *De* in the title is most often translated as "Virtue." The common English translation is "The Classic of the Way and its Virtue." By designating the book a *"jing"* Han dynasty scholars were judging it worthy of preservation in the Imperial Library. Many copies of this ancient text are in existence. However, since the printing of books was not known before the Tang Dynasty (618-906 CE), all ancient books were manuscripts individually copied. In the frequent re-copying of manuscripts errors occurred, and for this reason the various early texts of the *Dao De Jing* are not entirely identical word for word. These textual variations are the source of continuing scholarly controversies.

The *Dao Je Jing* first became known in the West in two Latin translations made by members of the Jesuit order at the beginning of the 18th century. The first European language translation was that of the French scholar Remusat in 1815. This was followed by a Russian translation in 1838, and the first English translation by John Chalmers in 1868. A selection of scholarly translations and commentaries in English appear in the bibliography section of this book. An extensive bibliography on works in Western languages relating to the *Dao De Jing* and "Daoism" can be found in J. J. Clarke's *The Dao of the West*.[2] For a bibliography of works in Chinese and Japanese see Wing-Tsit Chan's *The Way of Lao Tzu*.[3]

Prior to this century Western translations and commentaries have presented the philosophy of the *Dao De Jing* either from a religious perspective as transcendent metaphysics offering a vision of ultimate reality,[4] or from a philosophical and practical perspective as a handbook for political stagecraft in the service of empire. This division of interest and approach has roots in the early distinction in Chinese thought between *dao jiao* and *dao jia*, between religious Daoism and philosophical Daoism.[5] That the *Dao De Jing* is fundamentally a religious text is the position of Ellen M. Chen, whose translation and commentary appeared in 1989. In the Preface she says that "Tao points to an agricultural deity, not a warrior god," and that the *Dao De Jing* presents a vision of peace "grounded in a vision of the ultimate reality as non-being whose passivity and self-abnegation allow all beings to be." [6] A non-religious but mystical view of the *Dao De Jing* in found Arthur Waley's popular 1934 translation and commentary titled *The Way and its Power*. Waley presented the *Dao De Jing* primarily as a work concerned with the enhancement of the sage-ruler's power "to rule without being known to rule." [7] He described his approach as "historical" rather than "scriptural," meaning that it aimed to communicate the original meaning of the *Dao De Jing* rather than what the text may mean to contemporaries.

The translation and commentary offered in this book are historical in Waley's sense, but they develop a very different conception of the *Dao De Jing's* original meaning. Its teachings are presented as a coherent system of ecological thought that in all likelihood had its origin in an oral wisdom tradition associated with archaic sufficiency cultures. At the core of this system is a higher-order design for preserving the constancy of the life community and the pre-biotic environment on which it depends. The original wisdom of the *Dao De Jing* can be described, therefore, as a biocentric "political ecology" conceptualized and passed down by a tradition that practiced "the Way of the Sages" (DDJ 81).

This ancient wisdom with its concern for the constancy (sustainability) of the life community as a whole was brought forward during a time of crisis in pre-imperial Chinese civilization resulting from the disintegration of the Zhou clan confederacy and the feudal system it ruled. The collapse of this consanguineal state into warring kingdoms spawned a plurality of aggressive rulers with designs on imperial power. The *Dao De Jing* transmits the teachings of a naturalistic tradition recalled from an earlier era in order to counter these ambitions. This can be seen, for example, in passages that debunk the doctrine of the divine ancestry and sacredness of rulers, that reverse the anthropocentric concept of "great power" (by teaching that great power is non-designing, non-discriminatory, and sustaining rather than dominating), and that call on ruling elites to humble their ambitions, restrain their appetites, and preserve the self-ordering harmonies of nature, the natural flow patterns we now call ecologies.

The main teachings of the *Dao De Jing* are its holistic worldview,[8] its critical naturalism,[9] its revisioning of the concept of "great" power,[10] and its design for a political ecology that would put into practice the ancient sages' method of securing "constancy" (sustainability) by means of governance that "does not cut" (DDJ 28), but acts instead to benefit the life of a region by reining in the excessive design activities at work in the accumulation of power, wealth, and privilege.[11]

The translation and commentary presented in this book are an attempt to disclose the deeper layer of meaning the *Dao De Jing* has when it is read as conveying the holistic understanding of the world-process that the ancient sages' used to guide human designs toward simplicity and integration with nature and away from hierarchical instruments of domination. This interpretation is developed in conscious opposition to the long commentarial tradition, beginning with Han Fei (See Chan, *Sourcebook*, 251-61; Fung, *Short History*, 162-3), in which the critical, anti-imperialist thought of the *Dao De Jing* is neutralized and made compatible with and useful to the ideology of empire. The ever-popular Quietist wing of this commentarial tradition known as "Daoism," though it managed to preserve some of the oppositional nature of the text, is now the main obstacle to recovering its original meaning. This is due to the weight of its interpretation of key expressions, of which the set phrase *wei wu wei* is the leading example. In the interpretation developed in the translation and commentary of this book the Quietist tradition of Daoism is shown to be rooted in a misunderstanding of *wei wu wei* that results from the loss of the holistic perspective.

The *Dao De Jing's* holistic naturalism is founded on the "Constant Way" (DDJ 1). The Constant Way is a processive union of the opposites Being and Non-being, which are said to "arise together" (DDJ 2). It denotes a universal cyclical process called "great," (DDJ 25) because it is both the origin (DDJ 6) and the sustenance (DDJ 20) of the world. As a practical maxim the expression *wei wu wei* is intended to mirror this holistic union of opposites by joining the conscious design function of human action (*wei*) with the non-designed but self-ordering activity (*wu wei*) characteristic of the natural world. In this respect the *wei wu wei* maxim is both a recognition of the opposition between human action and natural activity and an injunction to preserve the unity necessary for a sustainable harmony between them. Rather than dominating and exploiting its "opposite" (natural activity), human action must unite with the non-designed process that underlies natural production, so as to benefit from it (DDJ 63, 64, 68).

The Daoist interpretation of the *wei wu wei* maxim is not holistic, and this is reflected in the various ways in which the *wu wei* part of the maxim is translated: as an adverb modifying the verb to act ("act non-coercively") or, less sensibly, as an object of the verb to act ("take or do no action"), or as the meaningless expression "act without action." These translations of *wei wu wei* are entirely about human action. They make the maxim a one-sided, reductive and anthropocentric expression. They do not recognize *wu wei* as designating the *activity* of the environing world that is not the work of conscious design. In its most mystical form the Daoist interpretation of the maxim is not even rationally anthropocentric. Its withdrawal from action altogether shuts down the most capable human response and therefore closes off the possibility of unifying opposites in an ecologically sustainable manner.

To recover the original meaning of the *Dao De Jing* we must put aside Daoism's penchant for the paradoxical and the mystical and read the work as a coherent body of thought whose foremost concern is the sustainability of the life-community as a whole. To say that the Dao can be lost (DDJ 38) is an epistemological recognition that the holistic paradigm of sustainability can be discarded and replaced by anthropocentric designs for domination that end in ruin (DDJ 29). The sages who practiced the Way in ancient times recognized this possibility and devised what may well be the world's first political ecology, a design intended to limit the use of state power to interventions that further and protect human communities and the natural life processes they are depend on.

THE TRANSLATION AND COMMENTARY

Except where noted the translation is of the Wang Bi text. The titles given to the individual verses are not part of the Chinese original. Titles should be read as concise summaries of the interpretation offered in the "Comment" section that follows the translations. Words or phrases in brackets added to the translated text are for the most part clarifying expansions necessary to complete a thought or idea, or to resolve an ambiguity. Usually these bracketed additions simply fill in omissions that are routinely permitted by the economy of classical Chinese. Karlgren wrote, "The Chinese sentence, compared with the European, is highly *brachylogical*. It reminds us most of the language used in telegrams, in which we have to express ourselves in as few words as possible." [12]

Brachylogical means brief, shortened, highly concise. The verses of the *Dao De Jing* use the economizing tendency of classical Chinese with poetic license, and this is the main reason that a "word-for-word" literal translation will not succeed in generating an accurate or coherent meaning. In large part this is because in the Chinese original punctuation is absent, pronouns are not marked for gender or number, and although Chinese distinguishes the function of nouns and verbs, there are no fixed "parts of speech" corresponding to them. Words are not inflected to indicate which is which.[13] Much of what we think of as grammar is handled in classical Chinese by word order and the use of particles which have multiple meanings. Word-for-word translation cannot deal with the ambiguity caused by such words except through selection, which presupposes a working interpretation. Hence, interpretation cannot be dispensed with. In some instances the bracketed additions I have added to the translated text are interpretative in a way that is explained in the comments. This is the case in those verse translations that diverge significantly from traditional ways of reading key passages (for example, DDJ 2, 3, 27, 32, 36, 37, 48, 49, 71 and 80). These verses and others are given further discussion in the "*Additional Comments*" section.

NOTES FOR THE INTRODUCTION

1. Hendricks, Robert G.: *Lao Tzu's Tao Te Ching,* 2000. Hendricks suggests 350 BCE as the year the Guodian bamboo slips were copied, but notes that they appear to be "copies" of "copies" (p. 22).

2. Clark, J. J.: *The Dao of the West,* 2000.

3. Chan, Wing-Tsit: *The Way of Lao Tzu,* 1963, adapted from chapter seven of his *A Sourcebook in Chinese Philosophy,* also 1963.

4. See, for example, Lin Yu-tang's comment in his *The Wisdom of Laotse* that Emerson's Transcendentalism is the best introduction to the *Dao De Jing.* He adds that Taoism is a philosophy of the unity and reversion "of all to the Primeval One, the divine intelligence, the source of all things" (pp 13-14). But what the text actually says is that all things return to Non-being, not to the One. Similarly, Blakney in the introduction to his poetic translation states that, "The Way corresponds to the Medieval conception of Godhead or Goodness...." (p. 38). Medieval Christianity never conceived of the Godhead as an impartial, non-designing natural process

5. See Fung: *Short History of Chinese Philosophy,* pp 211-212; Schipper: *The Daoist Body,* pp 184-87, 191-95; and *Schwartz, The World of Thought in Ancient China, pp 186-254.*

6. Chen, Ellen, *The Tao Te Ching*, p. x.

7. Waley's "historical" translation takes the position, mistaken in my view, that "*the Tao Te Ching* is not in intention...a way of life for ordinary people. It is a description of how the Sage (*sheng*) through the practice of Tao acquires the power of ruling without being known to rule" (p. 92). He locates the original meaning of the *Dao De Jing* in the shamanistic doctrine of a "magico-moral power" that can "shift Heaven and Earth." Kristofer Schipper's *The Taoist Body* continues the view that shamanism is "the substrate of Taoism," which, if true of the religious Daoism of *dao jiao,* is inconsistent with the philosophical naturalism of the *Dao De Jing*.

8. The original wisdom transmitted by the *Dao De Jing* is a form of holistic naturalism. Holistic thought sees humanity as immersed in a larger whole called Nature. In the intellectual world of ancient China the expression *tian xia,* literally meaning "under Heaven," was used holistically for the biosphere and the natural earth environment on which all life depends. The cosmos above and the earthly world "under Heaven" form the visible universe, the totality that the ancient holistic wisdom called "Being," or "the One." The "One" is not conceived anthropomorphically as a cosmic agent or designer, but is itself viewed as part of a larger whole called the Way (*Dao*), which is a universal process encompassing Being and the unseen opposite of Being, called Non-being. Non-being is said to be both the origin of Being and the "source" to which all beings return at the close of their existential careers. Because Non-being is the unseen origin and destiny of Being, the *Dao* as a whole is said to be unknowably dark and deep, and also beyond the scope for human comprehension. What is known about its "greatness" is the *constancy,* the unvarying stability, of its cyclical move-

ment between Being and Non-being, a process whose reliability dwarfs all anthropogenic efforts. The sequence of verses DDJ 1, 2, 16, 25 and 40 explains that the constancy of this cycle is such that it sustains without effort the visible totality, including the entire earthly world of "the ten-thousand things."

9. Naturalism in the *Dao De Jing* is similar to the naturalism that developed in ancient Greek philosophy, beginning with the Presocratics and continuing through the atomistic systems of Democritus and Epicurus. What is distinctive about the naturalism of ancient China is the addition of the concept of *Dao*, meaning "the Way," the cosmic *process* that encompasses both Being and Non-being. Ancient Greek naturalism lacks this proto-ecological concept. Throughout ancient materialism, and most Western philosophy as well, Non-being is a void, indistinguishable from empty space. Atoms move in the void but do not interact with it. In the original wisdom of the *Dao De Jing* Non-being is not conceived as a void, but as the "stillness" (DDJ 16) of an undifferentiated condition into which all durable things ("beings") pass when they can no longer maintain their integrity as coherent processes or living entities. The dissolution of all beings is said to result from a "weakening" (DDJ 40) that, like entropy, makes impermanence the fate of Being, so that all "beings" undergo reversal and return to Non-being, where, by an unknown process, Being is regenerated. What the naturalism of East and West have in common is their debunking of anthropocentric projections that turn natural occurrences into supernatural agents with both benevolent and malevolent intent. In the *Dao De Jing* natural order is seen as developing spontaneously from the interaction of the various "beings" that comprise "the One."

10. Early political formations in China, as elsewhere, were accompanied by the belief that great power was the power to dominate and that it was enhanced by a mystical quality that could be accumulated and passed to offspring. Hsu writes: "The nobles seemed to have believed that they possessed an inborn endowment that ordinary people did not have" (p. 20). See also Granet (pp.175-93 and 232-56). Elites looked on great power as the ability to control territory and obtain tribute. But with the development of the state system the idea of great power as domination gave birth to the mystification that the political ruler was the source of well-being for the entire life community. This mystification, institutionalized in the form of acts of ritual ("sacred rites") which only the ruler could perform (Gaster, p. 48), served to elevate a ruler's power above that of the Great Way's "power" to sustain, with the result that the human institution of rulership came to substitute itself for the Way as the sustainer of harmony in the world. Eventually, ruling elites reinforced their "greatness" by linking themselves to "divine hierarchies" (Wolf, p. 389). The Han dynasty went so far as to posit "an ideal correspondence" between the dynasty and Heaven and its constellations that gave the emperor and the state bureaucracy "a sort of supernal aura it might otherwise have lacked in view of the relative newness of the imperial state" (Henderson, pp 5-6).

In the *Dao De Jing* we have a record of the Wisdom tradition's effort to debunk the "greatness" of political power (and those who wield it) and to *reaffirm* the doctrine of "those good at practicing the Way in ancient times" (DDJ 15) that what is truly great is not the anthropic power to dominate, but the unseen "formless form" (DDJ 14) that stabilizes change by limiting and reversing extreme tendencies (DDJ 77). The *Dao De Jing* also says that this great sustaining "power" is without desire or designing action (DDJ 34, 37), and that lobbying efforts on the part of special interests are unable to sway it in their favor (DDJ 56). In the ancient Way of the Sages, great power is without desire, design or instrumental action, and is yet able to provide the basis of stable order that supplies sufficiency to the world as a whole. Great power, therefore, is *the power to sustain*, which the *Dao De Jing* calls *chang*, meaning "constancy," and attributes to the "Great Way" in the greatest degree.

11. The original wisdom of the *Dao De Jing* is the ecological wisdom of the ancient sages, who held to the holistic view that Being ("the One") is renewed as the result of the Way's cycling of Being through Non-being. According to this "enlightened" understanding, the natural world has constancy because it is part of this cyclical process. The universe of Heaven and Earth *is*, has sustainable existence, because the Way supports it with the constancy of its cycle of renewal. The fundamental problem confronted in the *Dao De Jing* is the "abandonment" (DDJ 18) and "loss" (DDJ 38) of this holistic perspective, seen in the contrast drawn in DDJ 77 between the "Way of Heaven" and the "Way of Men." The Way of Men reverses the holistic order of Being by treating it reductively. What in reality is the greater whole (tianxia, "the world") is partitioned into domains, pseudo-wholes carved out of "the One" by the dominating human power of rulership. Since the foundational design of this ruling power is the domination of a process whose constancy is holistic, rulers fail to see that the goal of domination cannot be realized and can only result in ruin (DDJ 29). The basis of all production in the world, even in the pseudo-wholes dominated by political rulers, is non-designed (*wu wei*) natural activity (DDJ 37). Political ecology in the *Dao De Jing* is the attempt to teach rulers that "Great governance does not cut" (DDJ 28), and that sufficiency and stability require that a ruler's governing acts (*wei*) protect

the greater natural activity supporting the life of a region. The meaning of the *wei wu wei* maxim (DDJ 3, 63), therefore, lies in the holistic understanding that the human community is embedded in and dependent on a greater whole and in the obligation this holistic understanding imposes on rulers to "gain unity" (DDJ 39) and care for the world (DDJ 13, 32, 37, 39, 48, 59, 64, 65, and 81).

12. *Sound & Symbol in Chinese*, p. 90.

13. For a scholarly discussion of the problems of translating the *Dao De Jing*, see the essay by Michael LaFargue and Julian Pas in *Lao Tzu and the Tao-Te-Ching*, pp 277-299.

.

DAO

1. The Constant Way

Ways we can speak about
are not the Constant Way.
Names we can assign
are not its constant name.
"Non-being" names
Heaven-and-Earth's origin.
"Being" names the mother
of the myriad things.

Therefore, ever without desire
observe the mysterious [origin],
and ever with desires
observe the limits [of things].
These two are the same
but differ in name.
Call them both profoundly
mysterious, and more mysterious
still—the gateway of all mysteries.

Comment: Being (the unity all "beings") and Non-being (the absence of "beings") are opposite poles of the cyclical process of change in the universe (DDJ 2, 14,16, 25, 40). The ancient wisdom tradition, the "Way of the Sages" (DDJ 81), taught that the *constancy* of this cosmic process is the basis for the stability and continuity of the world .*

2. The Unity of Opposites

All the world knows beauty as
being beautiful, thus not being
beautiful exists. All know good as
being good, so not being good exists.
Being and Non-being arise together.
Hard and easy complete each other.
Long and short shape each other.
High and low fulfill each other.
Voice and instrument harmonize.
Before and after form a sequence.
This is why people of Wisdom dwell
on matters of non-designing action
and go about teaching without words.

The myriad beings are active but
do not undertake [to act], produce
but do not take possession, function
but do not depend [on design and
control]. Gains are accomplished
but not laid claim to. Because there
is no laying claim, [gains] are not lost.

Comment: The ancient Wisdom tradition taught that the "constancy" of the universe (the continuance of stable conditions) depends on a balance between opposites that are said in this verse to "arise together," meaning that they complement each other and form a whole, such that an expansion or contraction in one registers an opposite effect in the other. What is not stated in this verse is the sage's recognition that human design activity is the complementary opposite of the activity that goes on in the natural world, and that an expansion of human design activity registers an impact in the world where stable order forms without any conscious design activity. Knowing this, the sages of the ancient Wisdom tradition are said here to "*dwell* " or "*stay with*" matters of non-designed activity. This is the opposite of what people usually do. The everyday activity of most adults is designed to support the flow of benefits from humanity's control of nature. Sages, on the other hand, draw attention to the constancy of the self-ordering processes of the natural world that are at risk of being diminished or lost as a result of excessive human design activity. What the ancient sages did, then, in "practicing the Way" (DDJ 15) was teach the community to correct the imbalance caused by designs for living that diminish the greater constancy of the natural activity which forms stable and productive order "on its own," without the need of design and control.*

3. Wisdom's Supportive Order

Not elevating the resourceful keeps
people from contention.
Not valuing hard to obtain goods
turns people away from theft.
Not viewing things that excite desire
keeps people's hearts and minds
from becoming agitated.

Therefore, Wisdom's order empties
hearts and minds and fills bellies;
relaxes wills and strengthens bones;
always draws people away from
the cleverness of [multiplying] wants,
and sees to it that clever individuals
lack the confidence to act.

Unite action with non-designed
activity. Then there is no disorder.

Comment: The disorders resulting from hierarchical design (hierarchy generates artificial scarcities) are contrasted with the supportive order that results from the harmonizing of human designs with natural activity and natural needs. Sufficiency is wisdom's counterbalance to excess on the one hand and artificial scarcity on the other. Reversal of extreme tendencies is the basis for stable sufficiency (DDJ 77). The design component of human action is limited by and balanced with the non-design of natural processes. Hence, *"there is no disorder."* *

4. The Unfathomable Depth of the Way.

The Way is a vessel that even with use
will not be completely filled.

Of such depth, it seems to be the ancestor
of all that is.

It blunts the sharp and unravels the tangled;
tempers the brightness and settles the dust.

Submerged [out of sight] it seems yet to be
preserved.

Whose child it is we do not know. It is older
than [the ancestral god] Di.

Comment: The origin of Heaven-and-Earth lies in Non-being (DDJ 1, 40)—
the obscure and unknowable *ancestor* of Being (and all the individual beings
that make up the world). It therefore takes precedence in the order of descent
over ancestral gods, like that of the Shang dynasty (1750-1100 BCE).

5. Impartiality and Impermanence

Heaven and Earth are impartial.
To them the myriad beings are straw dogs.
The sages are impartial.
To them the ruling clans are straw dogs.

Between Heaven and Earth is it not like
a bellows, empty but not caving in,
moving and supplying still more.
Much talk is taxing,
unlike remaining centered.

Comment: All beings without exception are "*straw dogs*." This metaphor derives from the use of straw figures in religious ceremonies. Afterwards "passersby trample on their heads and backs and grass-cutters take and burn them [as fuel] in cooking" (*Zhuangzi*, I, 352). Each being travels a path of entropy that ends in Non-being. The second stanza says the Way does not fail to supply more. This contrasts with those whose excess design activity causes enervating reversals ["caving in"] that result in deficiencies. To remain "*centered*" means to guard against the debilitating consequences of excess.*

6. Fecundity

The valley divinity does not die.
It is known as the mysterious female.
The mysterious female gate is called
Heaven's root. It appears to be
continuously re-stored.

Use it without strenuous effort.

Comment: In the ancient world the energies of nature were conceived as divine powers. Shamanism anthropomorphized these powers into spiritual beings. In the Wisdom tradition divinities are natural processes and potencies without personal identity, desire or conscious design activity. The female valley divinity symbolizes the procreative power of nature rooted in the constancy of the Way, which "*continuously re-stores*" to Being the productiveness that impermanence has removed. Because new beings issue from the same gate to which they eventually return, the mysterious female gate symbolizes the double movement of beings from and also back to their beginning in Non-being.

7. Reversal of Egoism

Heaven abides. The Earth endures.
The reason they endure and last long
is because they are not "self-born."
Therefore they can last long.

This is why those with wisdom are
self-effacing and the body of life
is advanced. They get beyond
themselves and preserve life.
Isn't it because they are not selfish
that they can complete themselves?

Comment: This verse implies that Heaven and Earth long endure because they do not cut themselves off from the source of constancy by pursuing self-genesis. Maturity and longevity depend on expanding "bodily life" to include the organic body of life as a whole. Holistic attainment requires a reduction in the pursuit of ego-gains (DDJ 38 and 48). Egoism negates this attainment by elevating the self above the whole (DDJ 22). Cultivating "self-effacement" liberates the body from the burdens of self-enhancement. The energy conserved by inner training contributes to personal longevity and supports the life design of oneness (DDJ 39), by which those with wisdom care for the world (DDJ 13).*

8. The Higher Good

The higher good is like water.
Water is good at benefiting
the myriad beings without
contending. It locates in
places generally disliked.
Thus it resembles the Way.

For dwellings, good is the earth.
For heart/minds, good is depth.
In giving, good is benevolence.
In speaking, good is sincerity.
In governing, good is order.
In practical affairs, good is
effectiveness. With action,
good is a matter of timing.

Since there is no contention
there is an absence of blame.

Comment: The higher type of good is said to resemble water, because water approximates the Way in its impartiality, its non-contention, and its humility in assuming the lower position— qualities that are cultivated by those of "higher attainment" (DDJ 38).

9. Extremes Are Not Sustainable

Grasping and filling up are not as good
as restraint. The effort to sharpen cannot
be sustained for long. A house full of gold
and jade cannot be kept safe. Wealth, rank
and arrogance are a sure path to self-ruin.

To make a contribution and then retire
is the Way of Heaven.

Comment: The wisdom of the Way follows the logic of sufficiency observed
in nature, referred to here as *the Way of Heaven*. When an excess of accumulation or deficiency reaches an extreme limit a reversal toward sufficiency
sets in (DDJ 77). The verse gives four maxims warning that reversal follows
excess. *"To make a contribution and then retire"* states the wisdom design for
doing what *"the Way of Heaven"* does naturally without design—namely, preserve the life-enhancing constancy of natural systems. The next verse (DDJ
10) shows that the ancient tradition cultivating this higher holistic attainment
practices a form of "inner training."

10. Profound Attainment

*In nourishing your physical nature and
caring for the One can you integrate [them]?
In concentrating your vital breath, can you
attain to the softness of an infant's?
In cleansing your hidden mirror, can you
make it free of all blemishes?*

*In loving people and reviving a region,
can you refrain from designing action?
When the gates of Heaven open and shut,
can you act as the female? Can you clearly
understand and make known the four
[principles] without taking action?*

*To produce and nourish,
but not for the sake of possession;
to act but not depend [on design];
to further without domination.
This is "profound attainment."*

Comment: The last stanza of DDJ 2 presented four principles that describe how the processes of nature work on their own without human design and initiation. In this verse the principles are re-stated with some variation and presented as the practical goal of a *profound attainment* that begins with inner training and finds its completion in the higher design of assisting "the self-ordering of the myriad things" without dominating them (DDJ 64).*

11. Non-being's Supportive Good

Thirty spokes together on one hub, but it is
vacancy [in the hub] that makes the cart useful.

Firing clay makes a vessel, but hollowness is
needed to make it useful.

Cut doors and windows in walls to make a room,
the empty spaces are needed to make it usable.

Therefore, Being serves the purpose of benefits,
Non-being serves [as a resource] for use.

Comment: The verse seems to be saying that Non-being has positive value. How can this be? The answer is that in the Wisdom tradition "Non- being" is not an abstract "absolutely nothing," but stands for the unseen origin of all that is. This vast resource supports the *"uncarved block"* of Being (DDJ 28), and is therefore the supportive good of all that is crafted from it to be of benefit. The three examples are not meant to illustrate a general principle. Axes, spears and walls are of benefit, but there is no empty space in them that makes them useful. Examples obscure the basic teaching, which is that what does not have form (Non-being) is a resource for the beneficial things that do.

12. Counsel Against Excess

The five colors make a person blind.
The five tones make a person deaf.
The five flavors ruin a person's palate.
Excessive gaming deranges a person's
heart and mind. Hard-to-get goods
hinder a person's movements.

This is why the [ancient] sages were
for the belly, not the eye. They let go
of the one and took hold of the other.

Comment: The ancient Wisdom tradition taught sufficiency as the balancing corrective to excess. Aspects of this "sufficiency ethic" are found in DDJ 3, 9, 15, 19, 24, 28. 29, 32, 44, 46, 65, 67, 77, 80 and 81.

13. Valuing Life above Rank

Favor, like disgrace, is distressing.
Rank is as great a worry as life.
Why say favor is distressing?
Favor confirms inferior status.
Getting it, like losing it, is distressing.
Why say rank is as great a worry as life?
We have major worries because we live.
Without life, what worries would we have?

Therefore, those who value life above rank
in their worldly designs can be entrusted
with the sheltering of the world.
Those who care for life more than rank
in their worldly designs can be entrusted
with the care and support of the world.

Comment: The inversion of values that gives rank more importance than life is countered and reversed by the Wisdom tradition. Ranks and the self-identities enhanced by them are subordinated to the higher-order value of caring for the world. The ecological soundness of this ordering of values was recognized by many pre-historical societies.*

14. The Ancient Way

Looked for but not seen it is called erased.
Listened for but not heard it is called rare
Grasped for but not gotten it is called minute.
These three cannot be further examined.
Therefore, they join in a single inquiry.

Its rising is not bright, its setting is not dark.
With a continuity that cannot be named,
it returns to "not-being-things."
It is called formless form, imageless image.
It is called vague and elusive.
Facing it you will not see its beginning.
Following it you will not see its end.

Hold to the Ancient Way to cope with
today's world. The ability to know the
earliest beginnings is called the
"leading thread" of the Way.

Comment: Sensory evidence does not reveal the source of constancy. What the senses confirm is impermanence and change (DDJ 5). And yet the world is not without "*a continuity that cannot be named.*" Stability and continuance are sustained by a dynamic "*formless form*" that gives rise to new things and incipient tendencies "*in today's world.*" The ancient Wisdom tradition counseled against expectations of permanence and developed a method for coping with change by following the "*leading thread*" of sufficiency and balance by which the Ancient Way sustains the continuity of the world.

15. Ancient Adepts of the Way

Those good at practicing the Way
in ancient times were so completely
subtle and profound that their
depth cannot be known. Therefore,
to describe them we must make-do
with appearances and say how they
were slow and deliberate, as though
they were fording a river in winter;
hesitant, as though fearful of those
on all sides; reverent, like guests;
yielding, like thawing ice, yet solid as
a block of wood; spacious as a valley,
yet opaque like turbulent water.

Who can quiet the turbulence and
gradually bring it to clarity?
Who can move what is inert and
gradually bring it to life?
Those who keep to this Way do not
desire excess. In the absence of excess
there can be ruin but also renewal.

Comment: Those in former times who knew how to practice the Way used the method of balance to avoid excess and preserve sufficiency. They were able to cultivate and employ both an active "yang" and a passive "yin" capability (DDJ 28) that enabled them to move the inert and quiet the turbulent, not by force, but by intervening early when shaping outcomes is still easy (DDJ 63, 64). Their wisdom, embodied in the maxim to unite action with non-designed activity (DDJ 3, 63), protected the world from excessive designs and enabled renewal in the event of ruin.*

16. The Meaning of Constancy.

Attain the utmost emptiness, secure
unbroken stillness. The myriad things
arise together and we watch their return.
Though they flourish in great numbers,
each returns again to the source.
Returning to the source is called "stillness."
Stillness is called "returning life."
Returning life is the meaning of constancy.
To know constancy is enlightenment.
Not to know constancy risks disasters.

To know constancy is to be tolerant.
To be tolerant is to be community-minded.
To be community-minded is to be holistic.
To be holistic is [join with] Heaven.
To [join with] Heaven is [to follow] the Way.
[To follow] the Way is to last long.
[Then] life is not in danger of extinction.

Comment: This verse contains a clear presentation of the ecological wisdom of the *Dao De Jing*. Its chain of definitions links contemplative awareness of the continuous cycle of Being's emergence from and return to Non-being to the Wisdom tradition's "profound attainment" (DDJ 10) in "practicing the Way" (DDJ 15) and in teaching (without words) how to care for the world. The sentence, "[Then] life is not in danger of extinction." is repeated in DDJ 52.*

17. Ruling Power and the Decline of Trust

In remote antiquity [rulers] were not known
to exist. In a later era, clansmen praised them
[as patrons]. Afterwards, they came to fear
them. In more recent times they came to
detest them.

Insufficient trust breeds distrust. Remote and
aloof, [rulers] put their trust in loyalty oaths.
Then, as deeds of merit occur and affairs are
proceeding, the clans all say, "We ourselves
[are responsible]."

Comment: Chiefs, the first to possess ruling power, were in the earliest societies mere figureheads, empowered on occasion to speak but not to command
(Clastres, 189-218; Kropotkin, 9-16; Wenke, 201). The establishment of
ruling power instigated competition for rulership, resentment among rivals,
declining trust, reliance on loyalty oaths, and presumption on the part of subordinate ranks. This verse provides an introduction to the next, in which the
political ecology that is part of the ancient Wisdom of the Sages is seen to
have been replaced by non-holistic cultural standards that valorize hierarchical ranking and give rise to hypocrisy and excess.*

18. When the Great Way Was Abandoned.

When the Great Way was abandoned, [the ideas]
of moral perfection and correctness appeared.

When [vulgar] wisdom and [clever] intelligence
arose, great hypocrisy and fabrication appeared.

When families were no longer united in harmony,
it was then one heard about filial [children] and
compassionate [parents].

When country and home [fell into] confusion and
disorder, "loyal" ministers appeared on the scene.

Comment: "The Great Way" refers here both to the Constant Way and the enlightened "Way of the Sages" [DDJ 81], which "follows" the Great Way by using the *wei wu wei* method to harmonize humanity's designs with the non-designed activity of the natural world. When the Great Way is abandoned, or lost (DDJ 38), the Way of the Sages is no longer the preeminent guide shaping human cultural and political designs. Instead, non-holistic doctrines are advanced that preserve the political and economic interests of various elite factions. The irony of the final line indicates that the so-called loyal ministers are maneuvering in a world of egoism, distrust, duplicity and stratagem.*

19. Counter-Ideology

Abolish the sacred, discard cleverness;
the people will benefit a hundredfold.
Abolish perfection, abandon correctness;
people will return to filial piety and caring.
Abolish craftiness, abandon profiteering;
robbery and thievery will cease to exist.

These three taken as a counter-ideology are
insufficient and need to be supplemented:
behold the plainness [of undyed silk];
embrace the naturalness [of unhewn wood];
be less selfish; have fewer desires;
leave off ritual studies; be free of anxiety.

Comment: This verse is a continuation of the previous two dealing with disorders arising from the quest for ruling power and the ideology that legitimates it. The counter-ideology developed in the *Dao De Jing* is aimed at debunking the doctrine that rulership is a sacred office supported by a hierarchy of clever individuals schooled in ritual behavior. It taught that the entire apparatus of the state created by such rulers is a structure of excess staffed by scholarly men who act as "guardians of the interests of great thieves" (*Zhuangzi*, Legge I, 289). Excess creates artificial insufficiencies and inner deficiencies. The second stanza offers two positive values, in symbolic form, as a guiding corrective.

20. A Wisdom Adept in the Courtly Crowd

How much do "yes" and "yea" really differ,
compared to the difference between good
and evil? One has to fear what everyone else
fears. What unending waste!

Those in the courtly crowd indulge them-
selves as though enjoying the "tai lao" feast,
or climbing up to a high terrace in spring.
I alone am unmoved, showing no sign.
Confused, like a new-born that has yet
to smile. Weary, like one without a home
to return to .

Those in the courtly crowd have everything
in excess; I alone seem to go without.
I have the heart-and-mind of a fool!
The common people show [themselves];
I alone remain obscure.
The common people are perceptive;
I alone [have my senses] sealed.
Restless like the sea, blown about endlessly.

Those in the courtly crowd all have their
use, while I alone am stubborn and abstain.
I alone am different from the others and
value taking sustenance from the mother.

Comment: The theme of the previous three chapters, "when the Way was abandoned," resonates here in the voice of a practitioner of the Way. From the viewpoint of those in the "courtly crowd" the ideal of simplicity embraced by the Wisdom tradition appears crude, primitive and foolish. In the eyes of the common people, whose lives are focused on work and family, the Wisdom adept appears "obscure" and set apart, without roots in village life. But it is from the courtly crowd that the alienation of this follower of the Way is most pronounced. The adept observes the cultivated life of the elite but "abstains" from joining in, and, possibly in the interest safety, gives no sign of his, or her, true feelings. The *Zhuangzi* says followers of the Way "reject the confusion of distinctions and ignore the differences of social rank" (Fung Yu-lan, p. 52). Aware of appearing rustic, backward and doltish, the speaker has chosen a life of honoring the Great Way, here referred to as "taking sustenance from the mother."*

21. The Way and its Continuity

The visible aspect of great attainment
is just going along with the Way.

How the Way becomes things is vague
and elusive. Elusive and vague, within it
are forms. Vague and elusive, within it
are physical things. Hidden and obscure
within it are seeds [of living energy].
These seeds are very real. Within them
there is promise [of continuity].

From distant antiquity to the present its
named [realities] have not died out. By
these we see the origin of the multitudes.
How do we know the origin of the multitudes'
form? Use this [continuity].

Comment: The ease and simplicity involved in "just going along with the Way" is contrasted with the conceptual effort required in seeking for assurance that the constancy of the Way's endowment of natural energies is continuous and therefore holds promise of future continuity.*

22. Wisdom Embraces Oneness

Bent yet whole, twisting yet true.
Hollow yet filled, worn away yet new.
Small yet gaining, ample but in doubt.
This is why sages embrace oneness as
the form of the world.

Not parading themselves, they enlighten.
Not being insistent, they become known.
By not cutting, their works have merit.
By avoiding self-importance, they gain
seniority.

The ancients say: "Bent yet whole."
Are these empty words? Surely, they
are complete, and one returns to them.

Comments: The ancient sages took the holistic view and embraced the unity of the world in its diversity. The unity of the whole is a unity of opposites. As DDJ 39 demonstrates with examples, oneness protects the constancy and continuity of the whole. By overcoming the partial view through the lens of the ego, they were able to see that the source of constancy is the stable pattern of life's renewal through death. While each "being" is bent toward return to Non-being, Being as a whole is sustained and continues. The *Zhuangzi* says that Enlightenment consists in seeing that "What makes my life a good makes my death a good also" (Fung Yulan, p. 99).*

23. Joining with the Way

Long-winded speech is not natural, for
a whirlwind does not outlast the morning;
a sudden thunderstorm does not outlast
the day. Heaven and Earth are the reason.
Since even they cannot [keep extremes
going] for long, how can human beings?

Therefore, those who join their undertakings
to the Way are one with the Way. Those who
attain [the Way] are one with [its] endowment.
Those who [join] with loss are one with loss.

The Way gladly gains those who join with it.
Its endowment gladly gains those who attain
to it. Loss gladly gains those who become
one with loss.

Comment: To join with the Way is to attain the equipoise of "being centered,"
a free response position the *Zhuangzi* terms "the pivot of the Way" (Mair,
14). To occupy the pivot enables one "to follow two courses at once" (Fung,
46) and to respond to change as needed in the interest of preserving harmony
and well-being by reversing extremes of imbalance. In this way the equilibrium necessary for life is guarded and loss can be avoided or minimized. The
Wisdom of the Way is therefore "an ecological achievement that is increased
or diminished by human participation and behavior" (Ames and Hall, p. 114).

24. Wasted Food and Needless Labor

Striding is not [good] walking, rising up
on tiptoe is not [a balanced way] to stand.
Parading the self does not enlighten,
being insistent does not distinguish.
The works of those who cut lack merit.
The self-important are not mature.

Those [who join] with the Way call these
"wasted food" and "needless labor,"
things universally despised. Therefore,
[those who] have the Way are not
involved [with such things].

Comment: Self-display, self-promotion, competitive aggression and vanity not only impede higher attainment, they contribute to stress, imbalance and exhaustion. The Wisdom tradition treats these as symptoms of egoism's mental disorder. The two metaphors of the second stanza link these symptoms to what we would now call eating disorders and obsessive-compulsive behavior. The expression "things universally despised" is repeated in DDJ 31 with regard to weapons. The position of the first two sentences of the Chinese text has been reversed in translation for rhetorical and poetic effect.

25. The Great Way

Something formed in chaos existed
before the birth of Heaven and Earth.
Vast and still, solitary and unchanging,
it moves in a cycle and is not in peril.
It can be thought of as the mother
of the world.

We do not know its name. If a word
is needed we call it "Dao." If we
have to name it we call it "great."
Great means passing [beyond].
Passing [beyond] means going far.
Going far means returning.

Therefore, the Way is great,
Heaven is great, Earth is great,
and Humanity is also great.
The world has four greats,
and humanity is one.
Humanity's law is Earth.
Earth's law is Heaven.
Heaven's law is the Way.
The Way is a law unto itself.

Comment: This verse restates in summary form the naturalistic understanding of the world developed in previous verses (DDJ 1, 2, 5, 14, and 16). Further clarification of this understanding occurs in DDJ 40 and 42. The first stanza states the paradox of a "thing" that precedes the natural world (Heaven and

Earth). It is said to be an indeterminate "chaos" that moves in an unchanging cycle, and therefore is said to stand still. The cycle consists in the emergence of Being from Non-Being (DDJ 40), followed by the return of each being to Non-being (DDJ 16). The "stillness" of this cyclical movement is the unvarying constancy of the process.

The word used for this unvarying cycle is "the Way," called "great" in the second verse. The third verse presents a simple schematic of "four greats," but it is clear that greatness consists in following the Way. Nature (Heaven/ Earth) is said to follow the "law" of the Great Way, while Humanity follows the law of the natural world. Unlike nature, however, Humanity deviates from the law of the Way by designing actions that weaken and degrade the constancy with which natural processes "of themselves" follow the Way. The Wisdom tradition sees this deviation as humanity's loss or abandonment of the Way (DDJ 18, 38). Humanity can be one of the four greats therefore only if it succeeds in doing by design what Nature does spontaneously and without design—namely, harmonize with the greater pattern of renewal that sustains Being and the living systems in nature.*

26. Two Practical Maxims.

Heaviness is the root of lightness.
Stillness is the ruler of restlessness.

Thus, the nobleman ending a day of
traveling does not leave his supply carts.

Even though there are scenic attractions
and a place to banquet he is unmoved.

How then can the lord of ten thousand
chariots behave any less seriously?

If one behaves lightly one loses touch
with the root. If one is restless one
loses control..

Comment: The maxims embody the order of values that the Wisdom tradition sees as essential for sustainability. "Heaviness" indicates greater value. The "root" refers to the origin of non-designed processes in nature. The actions designed by man are of less "weight" and importance. Therefore, to "*behave lightly,*" is to invert the order of values that gives humanity the assurance of constancy (sustainability), which is rooted in "stillness" (DDJ 16), the basis of natural activity. The maxims are illustrated with an example drawn from the life of a feudal nobleman traveling in the service of his lord.*

27. Transmission of the Light

Good walking doesn't trace footsteps
Good speaking doesn't censure flaws.
Good counting doesn't rely on tallies.
Good closing doesn't rely on lock and
key, yet what is closed cannot be opened.
Good tying doesn't bind with rope, yet
what is bound together cannot be undone.

This is why the sages were always good
at helping people and thus no one was
abandoned. They were always good at
rescuing, and did not abandoned things.
This is called transmission of the light.

So, those good [at practicing the Way]
are teachers of people who are not.
Those who are not adept [at the Way]
are a resource for those who are.
When teachers are not esteemed and
resources are not cared for, there may
be understanding, but it will be greatly
confused. This is an important subtlety.

Comment: The phrase "Transmission of the Light" and the following stanza
establish that the five sayings at the beginning of this verse are to be understood
in a teaching context. The sayings indicate that the Wisdom method avoids
imitative, instrumental, and mechanical technique in favor of creative adaptive responses that contribute to general sufficiency and non-abandonment.*

28. Great Governance Does Not Cut.

Know the masculine,
preserve the feminine.
Become a ravine in the world.
Serving as a ravine,
the constancy of your attainment
is not lost, and you return again
to [the holistic experience of] infancy.

Know the light,
preserve the dark.
Become an example in the world.
Serving as an example,
the constancy of your attainment
is not errant, and you return again
to the unlimited.

Know the exalted,
preserve the humbled.
Become a river valley in the world.
Serving as a river valley,
the constancy of your attainment
is sufficient, and you return again
to the naturalness of uncut wood.

Split and worked, uncut wood
is made into implements.
Wisdom adepts use its naturalness
in serving as senior officials.
For great governance does not cut.

Comments: In this important verse the ecological theme of stewardship is linked explicitly to the Wisdom tradition's political ecology. The poetic advance from stanza to stanza expands and deepens the meaning of the attainment that enables individuals with enlightened understanding to practice the Way in their lives, in their families, in their communities and when they assist in national government (DDJ 54). The verse concludes with a statement about the holistic character of "*great*" governance. In positions of power those who practice the Way "*do not cut.*" This gnomic statement should be understood in both its ecological and socio-political implications. "Not-cutting" means preserving the quality and constancy of the life-world. Socially and politically it means both providing for sufficiency while practicing non-abandonment (DDJ 27).

29. The Failure of Imperial Design

The desire to obtain the world
and make it [an object of design]
I see as an unattainable [aim].
The world is a divine vessel.
It cannot be made [an object of design].
Those who treat it in this way ruin it.
Those who grasp [for it] lose it.

For things either go or go along,
breathe a sigh or puff and blow.
Either strengthen or weaken,
either carry on or lose their grip.
So those with wisdom avoid excess,
extravagance and extremes.

Comment: The subject of this verse is the reversal of "great governance" (DDJ 28) by the type of designing action that attempts to substitute a hierarchical order of command and control for the spontaneous, self-organizing ecological order of the natural world, on which the hierarchical power structure itself is dependent. This, then, is a case of the tail attempting to wag the dog. What is in fact a dependency behaves as though it were an independent power. The failure of its design is evident in the outcome. The verse says: "Those who treat it in this way ruin it," meaning that the power of the whole is a "divine" *sustaining* power, while the imperial design is a *dominating* human power that ruins rather than sustains. By making the life of a region depend on a a center of commanding design, the goal of which is to extract grain-tribute from the subject populations, the land is stressed, labor is over-burdened and the constancy of natural productivity is weakened.

What is said to be unattainable is not utilization of nature to human cultural advantage. What is unattainable is the imperial domination of self-balancing natural systems without damage to the life-environment's innate capacity to produce a sustainable abundance. For this reason the ruin that follows on the imperial design forces human ecologies to increase the labor energy necessary to sustain a general level of sufficiency. This fact has a direct bearing on what is said in the final line, as was noted by Hsueh Hui in his commentary: "What Lao-Tzu means by 'extremes,' 'extravagances,' and 'excess' is not what people mean nowadays. The sage means whatever involves an increase beyond what is easy" (Red Pine, 59).*

30. Use of Force is Counterproductive

Those using [the Wisdom of] the Way
to assist a sovereign in governing do not
employ force of arms. This will likely
provoke the use of arms in return.

Where troops set up camp thistles
and thorns grow. Where great battles are
fought years of hardship will follow.

Those adept [in the use of the Way] do
not risk using force. They succeed with-
out vanity and without aggression, and
get results without arrogance, gain or
use of force.

When things strengthen they age.
It is said this is not the Way.
What is not the Way soon ends.

Comment: To age is to grow weaker is common knowledge. That making
something stronger ages and therefore weakens it is a more subtle observation.
It follows from the definition of strength as the power to resist and not to yield.
Such power shares characteristics with what is old—loss of the suppleness
and flexibility to adapt to change. What cannot survive change lacks the constancy that the Way is said to "lend" to things (DDJ 41). Here the maxim may
apply to a society organizing (strengthening) for war.

31. Weapons

Weapons are not instruments of good
omen. They are generally despised.
Thus those who practice the Way do
not involve themselves with weapons.

Since weapons are not instruments
of good omen, a noble person employs them
only as a last resort. A calm indifference
[toward weapons] is best. Victory [in
combat] is not a beautiful thing. Those
who glorify it exult in killing people.
Those who exult in killing will not
attain their aspirations in the world.

Comment: As a political ecology the wisdom of Way cannot rule out the use of military force. The second stanza emphasizes the difference between military preparedness on the one hand and what has been called a culture of "militarism" on the other.*

32. The Way Is Without Name or Rank

The Way is constantly without name or
rank. But even though it is uncrafted
and of small standing, there is nothing
in the world that can subjugate it.

If nobles and kings can safeguard it, then
the myriad beings will freely provide,
Heaven and Earth will unite in harmony
and rain down sweet dew, which people
will evenly distribute of their own accord
without being commanded to do so.

With a system of governance there are
names and ranks. And since there are,
we will also know to stop [their growth].
If we know to stop [their expansion]
we are able to avoid danger.

For the Way's presence in the world is
like a valley conducting rivers to the sea.

Comment: Contrast is a favored device of the Wisdom tradition. In ancient feudal society having a "name" meant more than a denotation. Name included rank and set royalty apart from the unranked "nobodies," who made up the bulk of the population. The verse is saying that the Way has the anonymity of the masses. If those who govern know how to limit the growth of the privileged and how to protect the unranked and unnamed then the community of life flourishes. If they do not, then life is in danger.*

33. Enlightened Self-Knowledge.

Those who know others are discerning;
those who know themselves are enlightened.
Those who defeat others have power;
those who conquer the self have strength.
Those who move forcefully have ambition;
those who know what is enough have
an abundance.

Those who do not lose their place endure;
those who "die" without losing their lives
are long-lived.

Comment: The verse returns to the theme of the cultivated attainment of those who understand that individual existence is a transient path and are able to act to protect the natural processes that support it. The final stanza contrasts those who endure by holding their place in the hierarchy with those who attain longevity by "dying" to fixed forms of social identity.

34. The Greatness of the Way

The Great Way floods forth. It can flow
left or right. The myriad beings rely on
it to live and it does not refuse them.
It accomplishes works of merit, but does
not take possession of them. It clothes
and feeds the myriad beings, but does
not act as their master. Constantly
without desire, it can be termed small.
The myriad beings return to it, but
as it is does not act as their master,
it can be termed great. As [the Way]
to the last does not make itself great
it is able to accomplish greatness. .

Comment: The Great Way is without desires. Unlike the feudal lords who take possession of the land and establish themselves as masters of those who work the land, the Great Way does not assert its "greatness" over the myriad beings of the world. The last two lines treat great power as the opposite of what it is understood to be in the consciousness of egoistic personality.

35. The Great Image

Holding the Great Image
the world goes forward.
Goes on and is not harmed,
tranquil in consummate balance.

Music and sweets entice,
passing guests linger.
But the words announcing the Way
are bland and utterly without flavor.

Watched for, it cannot be seen.
Listened for, it cannot be heard.
But in use, it cannot be exhausted.

Comment: The "Great Image" is the "formless form" of DDJ 14. This chapter continues the discussion by contrasting the sensory delights of music and sweets with the "flavorless" words that present the Way. When guided by the more profound attainment of the Way the world stays on an even course that is endlessly productive.

36. The Problem of Transmission

If one wishes something drawn in,
it must surely be stretched out.

If one wishes something weakened,
it must surely be strengthened.

If one wishes something brought down,
it must surely be lifted up.

If one wishes to take something,
it must surely be given.

This is called subtle understanding.
What is flexible and weak wins out
over what is firm and strong.

Fish cannot be removed from their pools.
A country's most beneficial asset cannot
be shown to people.

Comment: The verse opens with examples of opposites that reverse at the extremes of development. The understanding of this idea is called "subtle," and linked to a saying about the meaning of constancy (DDJ 30, 78). In the final stanza an analogy illustrates the problem of transmitting an understanding of how the Great Way sustains the universe of Being. Fish die when taken from the pools that are their natural habitat. Similarly, subtle understanding of the constancy of the Way, which requires a calm and receptive state of mind (DDJ 16), cannot be transmitted to those who are absorbed in worldly affairs (DDJ 41).*

37. Self-organization and Desire

The Way is constantly without
any action [of design], and yet
[natural] activity is not lacking.
If nobles and kings can protect
this activity, the myriad beings
will undergo self-alteration.

If in the process of alteration
desires become active we will
moderate them by using the
simplicity of the unnamed
and unranked. Truly, simplicity
is free of desire.

In the absence of desire there
is peace, and the world will
stabilize of its own accord.

Comment: The opening sentence says the Way does not design the world-process yet the world that emerges from the Way is not lacking in spontaneous activity capable of "order for free." How is this possible? In the Wisdom tradition stable order develops naturally from the fact that the myriad beings "arise together" (DDJ 16). In the first stanza the leadership ranks of society are called on to protect this naturally-occurring productive order from attempts to dominate it (DDJ 29).

The second stanza raises the problem of instability and conflict caused by a proliferation of desires. The natural world is without desires and the actions motivated by them, and yet it spontaneously forms stable order. By contrast, the human world is one in which desires in excess of what is needed to provide a minimum of sufficiency emerge and cause agitation, envy and disorder (DDJ 3). Practitioners of the Way are said to *act* with the design of "moderating" an upsurge of desire with the simplicity of the unnamed and unranked, meaning those who live their lives in simple sufficiency. The suggestion is that desires motivate the excess design activity that degrades the life-community, and that, like the sages of old who practiced the Way (DDJ 15), those who follow the Way will intervene (DDJ 63, 64) to assist the natural self-alteration of the myriad things that results in sustainable order based on the stabilizing principle of sufficiency (DDJ 46).*

DE

38. Higher Attainment

Higher attainment is not the attainment
of something more; it is [true] attainment.
Lesser attainment never stops attaining
something more; it is not true attainment.
Higher attainment is non-designing and
without intent. Lesser attainment acts
with both design and intent.

Higher benevolence acts with design
but has no [ulterior] aim.
Higher righteousness acts with design
and has an [ulterior] aim.
Higher ritual conduct acts with design
and when it gets no response, it rolls up
its sleeves and tosses out [those
who do not respond].

So, when the Way is lost there remains
[higher] attainment.
When [higher] attainment is lost, there
remains benevolence.
When benevolence has been lost there
remains righteousness.
When righteousness is lost there
remains ritual.

Those who [insist on] ritual conduct
are thin on loyalty and trust,
and this is the beginning of disorder.
Divining the future is trifling with

the Way and this marks the onset
of foolishness. This is why mature
people deal with what is substantial
and do not dwell on the trivial.

They deal with reality and do not dwell
on fantasy. They put aside the latter
and abide by the former.

Comment: The value of Higher Attainment is its freedom from the design to attain more. It functions therefore as a limiting paradigm. When the Way is lost (or abandoned), Higher Attainment may survive among a few (DDJ 70), who preserve the Way of the sages as a guide to curbing disruptive excesses and recovering the abundance based on natural sufficiency and balanced order. If this Higher Attainment is lost what follows is a downward spiral of ethical strategies ending in ritual conduct, loss of trust, disorder, and a disorientation that shows itself in the practice of divination and other types of "foolishness" that indicate the loss of a mature outlook on the world.*

39. The Importance of Unity

In time past these attained to unity:
gaining unity Heaven became clear;
gaining unity the Earth stabilized;
gaining unity the gods were spirited;
gaining unity the valleys were filled;
gaining unity the myriad beings lived
[and reproduced]; gaining unity nobles
and kings acted with correctness in the
world. [All] this came about [by unity].

If Heaven were not thus clear [we] would
dread its rupture; if Earth were not thus
stabilized [we] would dread its quaking;
if the gods were not thus spirited [we]
would dread their cessation. If valleys
were not thus filled [we] would dread
their desiccation; if the myriad beings
were not thus productive [we] would
dread their extinction; if nobles and
kings were not thus correct [we] would
be in dread of setbacks.

So, the exalted has the humble as its root;
the higher has the lower as its foundation.
Thus, nobles and kings call themselves
orphans, wretched ones, and paupers.
Isn't this taking the humble as the root?
What has the most renown lacks renown.
This is the reason for not desiring finely-
carved jade over unpolished stone.

Comment: In DDJ 10 and 22 unity or "oneness" is presented as a cultivated attainment. Adepts of the Way are said to embrace, or join with, the One. For poetic effect and symmetry this verse makes it appear that natural things do the same— attain to unity. But DDJ 42 says that natural things are part of the unity of Being ("the One") from the first. They evolve a unity as functionally coherent beings, but this process differs from the cultivated oneness attained by people of wisdom or the "nobles and kings" who are said to have "gained unity" and "acted with correctness in the world." The Way of the Sages is a design for attaining to oneness by uniting with natural processes, which "gain" oneness spontaneously without the purposeful action of design. Although the processes differ, the Wisdom design is to obtain the same result— constancy and stability that is supportive of the life-world as a whole. The main teaching of the verse says the attainment by ruling elites in upholding oneness is meant to protect the ecological conditions of a sustainable life-world, and that in the event that they fail to be holistic in their thinking and in their governance there is reason to fear "setbacks" in the life-world and in the quality of the environment it is dependent upon. "What has the most renown lacks renown" repeats the Wisdom tradition's reversal of the established values of vertical civilization, where value (hierarchical rank and reputation) is linked to the accumulation of power and wealth. The Way of the Sages teaches that what has the greatest value is without renown because it lacks name and rank, has no social standing (DDJ 32) and is laughed at (DDJ 41) by those whose ignorance is the result of a cognitive disorder (DDJ 71).

40. How the Way Works

Reversing is [how] the Way moves.
Weakening is [how] the Way functions.
The myriad things of the world are born
of Being. Being is born of Non-being.

Comment: The Great Way is sustained by cyclical movement (DDJ 25). Reversal and return follow on the weakening of each thing's initial endowment. "Being" is therefore a transitory process that "runs down." Loss of constancy, integrity, and the potency to resist dissolution return all beings to Non-Being. The "myriad things" trace a curvature of entropy from the fullness of potency (DDJ 55) through a decline that eventually ends in death (DDJ 50). They are born of the unity of Being and their life movement is one of return to Non-being. But if return to Non-being were the whole story, the Way would not be continuously supportive, and life would therefore be in danger of extinction (DDJ 16, 39). The Wisdom tradition saw the cycle of the Great Way as a "double movement" (DDJ 6) in which return culminates in renewal. The renewal phase of the cycle is called "stillness" and "returning life" (DDJ 16). This accounts for how there can be both damage and ruin but also renewal (DDJ 15). Being and the things that evolve from it have their origin in Non-being. But how it is that the stillness of Non-being renews Being remains unknown. The renewal phase of the Great Way is dark and inscrutable (DDJ 4).

41. Three Types of Scholars

When scholars of the first rank
hear about the Way, they zealously
institute it. When average scholars
hear about the Way, they seem at times
to hold to it and then at other times to
lose it. When inferior scholars hear
of the Way, they roar with laughter.
If they didn't laugh it wouldn't qualify
as practicing of the Way.

Thus, we have the established sayings:
The clear Way seems obscure.
The advancing Way seems to retreat.
The smooth Way seems uneven.
Higher attainment seems like a valley.
Great purity seems defiled.
Wide attainment seems insufficient.
Vigorous attainment seems listless.
Substantial truth seems inconstant.
The great square is without corners.
The great implement is the last completed.
The great note sounds thin.
The great image is without form.

The Way is hidden and unnamed, yet
it is good at lending [its constancy] and
completing [things].

Comment: The scholars here are the shi4, men of cultivated abilities who served the rulers of the various states. The verse parodies their varying responses to the Way and the Wisdom based on it. The shi4 of the first rank fail to see that one models the constancy of the Way by balancing opposites, not by seeking to institute more executive control

42. Sustainable Harmony

The Way generates the One.
The One generates Two.
Two generates Three .
Three generates the myriad beings.

The myriad beings carry yin and
embrace yang, fusing vital breaths
to create [sustainable] harmony.

What people hate is to be orphaned,
wretched and impoverished. Yet kings
and dukes take these as their titles—
since things are either lessened by
increase or increased by reduction.

What others teach we also teach.
Those who force the beam do not die
a [natural] death. We should take this
as the father of our teaching.

Comment: "The One" indicates Being as renewed by Non-being. The Two, Three and the myriad beings appear to symbolize stages in the self-differentiation of the original stem-cell of Being. Traditionally, the Two referred to yang and yin, symbolized in the *Yi Jing* (*I Ching*) by Heaven (activity) and Earth (potency). Three is said to produce the myriad species and individual beings and is thought to stand for Heaven, Earth and Humanity, taken together as the creative forces of Nature. The second stanza says in the live being yin and yang energies take the form of " breaths" that fuse harmoniously. The yang "breath" of actively expending energy is followed by the yin "breath" of drawing in and replenishing the yang expenditure. This harmonious alternation of expenditure and replenishment follows the supporting cycle of the Way. From the point of view of the myriad beings then the Way can be said to "lend" (DDJ 41) its constancy.

The final stanza repeats the ancient Wisdom tradition's warning about excess—in this instance about the harmful consequences of extreme actions that "force the beam." Such actions weaken the fusion of vital breaths and the constancy "lent" the life-community by the Way. Loss of harmony, therefore, has an impact on longevity. For this reason those who by their extreme actions "force the beam" are said to forfeit a natural death.*

43. The Benefit of Non-Design

What is most pliant in the world
gallops over what is most firm.
What has no being enters where
there is no crevice. This is how
we know the benefit of non-design.

Teaching without words,
benefiting without design,
few in the world attain to these.

Comment: The Great Way is ever without design activity (DDJ 37). Its benefit for humanity and for all life is the reliability of its cycle of return and renewal. The first stanza re-works the teachings of earlier verses: the Way moves through the world like a (silent and unseen) flood. Although little noted and nameless, its power is such that nothing can subjugate it. The Wisdom of the Way emulates the constant and beneficial movement of the Great Way with practices that are in harmony with the spontaneous, non-designed processes of natural order that humanity and all life are dependent on.

44. The Freedom of Sufficiency

A name or your life, which is closer?
Your life or your property, which is
the more [dear]? Gaining or losing,
which is [more] debilitating?

Extreme attachment comes at great cost.
Excessive storing brings a burden of loss.

Thus, to know sufficiency frees one from
disgrace; to know when to stop frees one
from danger and enables one to continue
for a long time.

Comment: The verse opens with questions that seem merely rhetorical. Life and well-being are a necessary condition for enjoying fame or possessions, but the attraction of the latter is so strong that lives have been wrecked in the pursuit of them. The third question links excessive attachment to fame and property with loss of mental and physical well-being, which can be prevented by the wisdom of sufficiency, referred to as knowing "how to stop" (DDJ 32), knowing "sufficiency" (DDJ 33) and knowing "what is enough" (DDJ 45).*

45. Stillness Rights the World

Great achievement seems lacking,
yet its usefulness does not wear out
Great abundance seems to abate,
yet its usefulness is not exhausted.
Great straightness seems crooked.
Great skill seems clumsy.
Great argument seems to stammer.

Agitation overcomes cold.
Tranquility overcomes heat.
Complete stillness rights the world.

Comment: The ancient wisdom tradition confronted the fact that for most people what is great is the power to dominate. The Wisdom of the Way seems
"mystical" because it teaches instead that what is really great is the "power"
of the Way to sustain the continuity of existence without any action to design
to shape outcomes. Complete stillness rights the world by allowing the world
to form a stable equilibrium "of its own accord" (DDJ 37).

46. The Adequacy of Sufficiency

When the world has the Way,
the war horses of the nobility
are returned to manure the fields.

When the world is without the Way,
the nobility's war horses
are bred outside [the walls of their towns].

There is no harm greater than not knowing
what is enough.
There is no fault greater than desiring gain.

Knowing the adequacy of what is enough is
constantly sufficient.

Comment: This verse links the ethic of Sufficiency to the Wisdom tradition's ecology of renewal. The pasturing of the nobility's horses to fertilize fields is an example of the "return" required for sustainable agriculture. This "renewal" was impaired when the horses used in war were corralled and bred outside the walled towns of the nobility. The "fault" in the desire for gain is that of excess beyond "what is enough" to assure the balance required for sustainability.

47. The Path to Enlightenment

Understand the world
without going out of doors.
See the Way of Heaven
without looking outside.
The farther one goes,
the less one knows.

Sages comprehend without
traveling about; have an
enlightened perspective
without taking in the view,
and achieve [beneficial results]
without designing actions.

Comments: The verse is a teaching about the path to enlightenment, said here to be hindered by external forms of seeking. Travel in the real or virtual world gathers a fund of information, but the activity involved obstructs "complete stillness" (DDJ 45), which yields insight concerning the Way (DDJ 16) and its constancy in supporting Heaven and Earth without domination or design activity. What is achieved without designing action is the higher good of DDJ 8 (impartiality, non-contention, and humility) which makes possible the Higher Attainment of DDJ 38.

48. Obtaining the World

To study a subject add to it every day.
To practice the Way cut back every day.
Cut back again and again until you are
not acting by design. In not acting by
design [you see] that [natural] activity
is not lacking.

Obtain the world always by not taking
up the task. Reaching for it by taking
up the task doesn't obtain the world.

Comment: The first stanza recounts the teaching of earlier chapters (DDJ 2, 3, 10, 16, 23, 29, 30, 37, 38, 43). Natural activity is spontaneously productive and functions at its optimum when it is free of human designs to control it. But how then can the world to be obtained? The wisdom tradition's seemingly paradoxical reply is that the world is "*obtained*" by giving it the respect that protects it from human designs (DDJ 29) likely to degrade its productive abundance. It is this gift of abundance that is obtained by protecting the source, the natural activity of living beings functioning together on their own, without any acts of design and control.*

49. Sages Are Impartial

Sages are always impartial.
They take the attitude of the ruling
clans as [an example of] partiality.

Those of worth we accept.
Those lacking worth we also accept.
Attainment means acceptance.
Those who are trustworthy we trust.
Those not trustworthy we also trust.
Attainment means trust.

In the world sages withhold [judgment].
Acting in the world their hearts and
minds are simple and guileless.
The ruling clans all focus their ears and
eyes on them, and the sages regard them
as children [in need of guidance].

Comment: The ruling clans possessed an elitist psychology at odds with the Way. Their belief system claimed descent from an ennobling "immortal" ancestor (Hsu, pp 19-20). They shared the common bond of a hereditary right to rule based on a transparent psychological fiction, which is debunked in DDJ 5. Here the intent is to contrast the tolerant, holistic psychology of those following the Way of the Sages with the discriminating and judgmental mentality of the clan elites. This may explain why those following the Way regard them as children who lack the maturity to govern with greatness.*

50. Three in Ten

Emerge into life, enter into death.
The partisans of life are three in ten.
The partisans of death are three in ten.
Three in ten also are those who push
life toward death spots. Why? Because
they [seek] to consume more of life.

We hear that those who are good at
conserving life do not encounter a tiger
or rhinoceros [in unfamiliar] lands.
If they enter battle without protective
armor and weapons, a rhinoceros has
nowhere to thrust its horn, a tiger has
nowhere to fasten its claws; weapons
have no leeway [to thrust in] their blades.
Why? Because they have no death spots.

Comment: If 3 in 10 is a way of saying 1/3, as the Wang Bi commentary has it, there remains 1 in 10 not identified. This remainder could refer to a much smaller group that is "good at conserving life," an appropriate description of those who follow the Way of the Sages and, by knowing what is enough, are thereby able to avoid losses. This implies that the majority of people fail to conserve life because in their effort to "consume more of life" they undertake actions that tempt death. Unwise risk-taking makes them more vulnerable and may be what is meant by the expression "death spot."

51. The Way Gives Life

The Way gives life to the myriad things.
Its endowment rears them, matter forms
them, circumstances complete them.
This is why the myriad beings do not
fail to honor the Way and esteem its
endowment. They honor the Way and
esteem its endowment not by decree,
but always of their own accord. Thus
the Way gives them life; its endowment
fosters, increases, nurtures, shelters,
nourishes, supports and covers them.

To produce but not hold on to;
to act but not depend [on design and
control]; to enhance but not dominate—
this is called profound attainment.

Comment: In the productive phase of the Way's cycle the myriad things receive an endowment of potency that carries them through their own life cycles. DDJ 34 says the Way clothes and feeds the myriad beings, but does not act as their master. Their mutual "arising together" (DDJ 16) and the harmony and constancy of their fusion of "vital breaths" (DDJ 42) is spontaneous and without design. In the first stanza of this verse the subject is the Way and the endowment of potency it gives the myriad things. The subject of the second stanza is the "attainment" of the Wisdom to practice the Way. The aim of this practice is not to make private gains but to prevent degradation of life's capacity to flourish and reproduce (DDJ 28, 29).

The Wisdom tradition teaches the method of *wei wu wei*. This set phrase calls for human design activity to be united with the non-designed processes of nature in a way that respects the greater life-enhancing constancy of the latter, which "maintain the availability of all substances critical to life" (Van der Ryn and Cowan, p. 106). Followers of the ancient Way of the Sages sought to harmonize culture with nature by integrating human designs with nature's non-designed processes, so as to safeguard the restorative cycle that gives constancy to natural systems.*

52. Safeguarding the Mother

The world has a beginning and it
serves as the mother of the world.
Gaining mother, we thereby know
her children. Knowing her children
we can in turn safeguard the mother,
and the body of life is not in danger
of extinction.

Block the openings, close the doors,
and to the end life will not be toil.
Open the gates, enhance activities
 and to the close life will not be
relieved [of toil].

We call seeing the small enlightenment.
We say safeguarding the weak is strength.
Use the light [of example] to restore
enlightenment. Not to leave life a legacy
of ruin is to weave the pattern of constancy.

Comment: The explicit concern for the safety of "the mother" (DDJ 20) in the first stanza confirms the Wisdom tradition's holistic view of the body of life (DDJ 7). The rest of the verse comments on practicing constancy to protect the body of life from extreme designs (DDJ 29) and governance that cuts (DDJ 28).*

53. By-passing the Way

If we have some knowledge of walking
the great Way, using it should be the only
concern. The great Way is very level
and safe but people are fond of bypaths.

The ruling houses deduct too much, the
granaries are empty and the fields are
overgrown with weeds. At court they wear
richly designed silk clothing, carry weapons,
gorge themselves with food and drink, and
have an excess of wealth and possessions.

This is called "robbers boasting."
It is certainly not the Way!

Comment: In the first stanza "by-paths" is a figure of speech for actions that deviate from the Way's pattern of balance based on sufficiency. The ruling elite create artificial scarcities and hardships by their extravagant life-style. The observation that excess appropriation of grain by the ruling houses leaves agricultural villages under their sway with less than enough food for survival is repeated in DDJ 75.

54. Transgenerational Continuity

What is well established is not uprooted.
What is firmly embraced is not stripped
away. Sacrificial offerings by sons and
grandsons do not end.

Cultivate it in oneself and the attainment
will be genuine. Cultivate it in the family
and the attainment will be all-sufficing.
Cultivate it in the village and the attainment
will be lasting. Cultivate it in the nation
and attainment will be overflowing.

Therefore, use one's own [perspective]
to see another's. Use the family's to see
[that of other] families. Use the village's
to see [that of other] villages. Use the
country's to see [that of other] countries.
Take up the global [perspective] to see
that of the whole.

How do we know the world is so?
By means of this.

Comment: A well-established Wisdom practice binds past, present and future together in a trans-generational continuity that gives meaning to the idea of constancy, or in the language of modern ecology, sustainability.*

55. *Natural Endowment in Its Fullness*

Retaining natural endowment in its
fullness would make one similar to
a newborn infant. Poisonous insects
do not sting it. Wild animals do not
attack it. Predatory birds do not seize
it. Its bones are weak, its muscles soft
but its grasp is firm. It knows nothing
of sexual union but its little organ
stirs—the utmost in living energy!
It can wail all day without growing
hoarse— the utmost in harmony!

Knowing harmony we call constancy.
Knowing constancy we call enlightenment.
Benefiting life we call auspicious.
Mind ordering the vital breath we call
compulsion. Strengthening things soon
ages them. We say this is not the Way.
What is not the Way has an early end.

Comment: The pre-cultural condition of infancy is the stage of human life closest to the Way. At this stage a person's natural endowment of potency is at its fullest. The infant is therefore said to have the harmony of living energy to the utmost degree. After fanciful examples of infant invulnerability, the harmony of living energy is linked to constancy and attainment of enlightened understanding. Benefiting life means protecting the harmonious balance of opposites within it. Those attempting to dominate life's "vital breaths" by exerting control over them disrupt the holistic harmony of the body and the environment in which these "breaths" are "fused" (DDJ 42).*

56. Profound Union

Those who understand do not talk.
Those who talk do not understand.

Block up the openings; close the gates.
Blunt the sharp-pointed; separate the
tangled; soften the glare; settle the dust.
This is called profound union.

There is no being closely or distantly
related [to the Way]. There is no profit-
ing or [suffering] injury from it. There is
no being ennobled or debased by it. For
this reason it is honored by the world.

Comment: This verse continues the theme of self-cultivation found in earlier verses: DDJ 7, 10, 16, 28, 47, 48 and 52. The goal of this discipline is to "attain" union with the Way (DDJ 10) by becoming "a valley to the world" (DDJ 28) and helping things "return one after the other to the Great Succession" (DDJ 65). The final stanza reinforces the earlier teaching about the Way's neutrality (DDJ 5), adding that this is why it is honored by the world.*

57. Lesson in Governance I

In governing a country use normative
order; in fielding an army use surprise.
Obtain the world by not taking up the task.
How do we know this? By the following:
The more taboos in the world, the poorer
the people; the more instruments of profit,
the more confusion there is in the land.
The more clever and tricky the population,
the more extraordinary incidents occur.
The more laws and edicts are decreed,
the more robbers and thieves there are.

Therefore, the wise [ruler] says: I am
without designs [on the world] and people
transform themselves. I prefer tranquility
and people themselves establish order.
I am not involved in business affairs, and
the people themselves create abundance.
I have no desire [for gain], and the people
themselves cultivate a life of simplicity.

Comment: As in previous verses, guarding and furthering harmonious order in society and in society's relation to natural processes requires governance that "does not cut." This and the following verse offer lessons in this type of governance .*

58. Lesson in Governance II.

When government is unobtrusive,
the common people are simple
and honest. When government
is prying and invasive, the people
are deficient and needy.

Misfortune is what good fortune
leans on. Good fortune is where
misfortune hides. Who knows the
[limiting] extremes? There is no
[set] rule. Order turns to disorder.
Good turns to evil. The day of the
people's confusion is long indeed.

This is why wise [rulers] square
but do not cut; join [opposites]
but do not injure; straighten
but do not strain; are luminous
but do not dazzle.

Comment: The proper historical context for the philosophy of wise government in the *Dao De Jing* is the period of ancient China's clan-based domination of self-sufficient agricultural communities. The assumption of self-sufficiency is what makes the opening statements of this chapter (and those in DDJ 57 and elsewhere), a coherent philosophy of government. It is a serious mistake to apply this view of how government should work to societies of the modern capitalist era, where, for the most part, self-sufficiency has been replaced by a highly integrated global market mechanism that requires extensive government subsidies and governmental regulation in order to continue functioning. The second stanza introduces the "confusing" issue of cosmic justice, which is beyond the ability of even great governance to address. (See also, DDJ 73). The concise lessons on wise government in the final stanza are obscure and interpretations of them vary widely. The teaching that government must be restrained and non-invasive is continued in DDJ 65 and in the sequence 72-75.

59. Political Ecology I

In governing people and looking
after nature there is nothing like
conservation. Only conservation
is called early service [to the Way].
Early service [to the Way] restores
our endowment. If we re-store this
endowment, we are not disabled.
If we are not disabled, then our limits
are not known. If our limits are not
known, then we can have a country.
If we have the country's mother, then
we can last long. When it is said,
"Deep roots, sturdy roots" this is
the way of long life and lasting insight.

Comment: Ecological and political themes are unified in the Wisdom tradition's holistic teaching of sustainability, good government and transgenerational continuity. Where culture merges with nature—e.g., in agriculture—
design merges with non-design, and takes the form of care and husbandry.
Renewal of the life-world's natural endowment prevents the development of
incapacities that weaken. The last lines add that protection of the country's
"mother" (DDJ 52) is a condition for the country's longevity.*

60. Lesson in Governance III

Rule a large country like you cook
small fish.

When the Way governs the world
demons do not have divine power.
Not only do demons lack such power,
their power does not harm people.
Not only does their power not harm,
wise [rulers] also do not harm people.
And if these two do not cause harm
to one another, then [a country's]
endowment unites and returns.

Comment: The verse opens with a famous analogy. Just as cooking small fish requires gentle handling, governing a large country requires attention to the needs of its weaker and smaller components. Rulers who follow the Way "do not harm people." They transcend the egoistic motives that underlie evil actions and bring hardship upon the life community. The Wisdom of the Way is to "act" without contention (DDJ 81). Where there is no contention a community's gains are not lost. The Wisdom based on the Way is naturalistic. What is "divine" (i.e., deathless) has neither designs nor agency. Demons do not have divine power because they are imaginary beings. Therefore, "their power does not harm people."

61. Lesson in Governance IV

The large country flows lower. It is
the world's [place of] intercourse,
the world's female. The female always
uses tranquility to win over the male.
By means of tranquility [the female]
takes the humbler [position].

Therefore, through humility the large
country makes an ally of the small
country. And it is through humility
that the small country gains the large
country's support. Thus, it is through
humility that large countries make
allies and small counties gain support.

A large country wants to hold
together and provide for its people.
A small country wants to enter into
exchange with others. Since each of
the two gains what it wants the large
country properly humbles itself.

Comment: The previous verse dealt with internal affairs. Here the topic is foreign relations. The Wisdom of the Way's concern with harmony achieved through *non-contention* is evident, as is the bilateral principle of exchange for the common good.*

62. The Way Is a Storehouse

The Way is the myriad things' storehouse.
Treasured by those who are adept at
following the Way, it sustains those
who are not good at following the Way.

Beautiful words can buy honor.
Fine conduct can enhance one's status.
How then can people not so valued be
abandoned? Therefore, when enthroning
the Son of Heaven and installing the three
ministers, it is not as good to be the bearer
of jade disks before a team of four horses
as it is to kneel in presenting this Way.

Why did the ancients honor this Way?
Did they not say, "Seeking for gain
is a fault to be avoided?" Therefore,
[the Way] is honored by the world.

Comment: As standards of worth, honoring ruling elites rather than the Way narrows the category of value and serves to obstruct rather than facilitate constancy and harmony. The holistic wisdom founded on the Way reverses the ruling conception of value in its design for integrating human practices with the greater sustaining value of what is "uncrafted and of small standing" and without name and rank (DDJ 32). It is the non-designed harmonies of nature that provide human communities with a stable and sustainable "order for free."*

63. Wei Wu Wei I

Unite action with non-action;
be of service to the unserved;
taste what is without flavor;
[regard] the small as great;
[make] much of the minor.

Plan the difficult when it is easy.
Manage the big when it is small.
The world's difficult business must
start from the easy. The world's
major works must start with minute
details. This is why the sages did
not in the end act great yet were
able to accomplish what is great.

For those who promise lightly will
surely gain little trust; those who treat
things as easier than they are will surely
make them more difficult. Therefore,
the sages treated things as difficult
and thus did not end up in difficulty.

Comment: The Way of the Sages is an ecological design for preserving or recovering harmony by the unification of opposites. Following the Way's pattern of constancy weaves the designs of human activity into the stable non-designed processes of the natural world. Five maxims in the first stanza present koan-like summaries of the teachings of previous verses: unite human action and the non-designed activity that occurs in nature (DDJ 3, 37); expand the range of human concern (DDJ 7, 10, 28, 51, 54, 59); expand the range of human experience (DDJ 16, 21, 47); reverse preconceptions about value and rank (DDJ 13, 34, 39, 62); reverse preconceptions about what is important (DDJ 26, 32, 41).

The second stanza counsels that maintaining balance based on natural sufficiency requires early intervention. The harmonizing design that protects constancy calls for intervention in the on-going flux of change. It combines a recognition of the increased burden of doing nothing with an understanding of the benefits that flow from an early response. What is great can be preserved without great undertakings because what is truly great is the harmony and constancy of the myriad things that flourish on their own without the need of design and effort. Adaptive intervention to preserve this greatness is the meaning of the *wei wu wei* maxim to unite design with non-design, and also the meaning of the ancient sages' holistic principle (DDJ 15) to "practice the Way" (*wei dao*). The "higher attainment" (DDJ 38) required to protect the well-being of the least of things makes intervention difficult from the beginning.*

64. Wei Wu Wei II

What is stable is easy to sustain.
What is not yet seen is easy to plan.
What is brittle is easily shattered.
What is minute is easily scattered.
Act on things before they unfold.
Manage them before they boil over.
A tree you can wrap your arms
around grows from a seedling.
A terrace of nine levels rises from
a shovelful of earth. A journey of
a thousand miles begins with a step.

Those with designs on things ruin
them. Those who grasp for them lose
them. Therefore, the sages did not have
designs on things and therefore did not
ruin them. They did not grasp for things,
and thus did not lose them. When people
engage in business it is always when
success is near that they come to ruin.
By taking as much care at the end as at
the start one does not ruin one's work.

Therefore, the sages desired what was
not desired and did not desire goods that
were hard to obtain. They learned what
was not learned, and went back to what
others had passed over. They assisted
the self-ordering of the myriad things
and did not dare to act on them. *

Comment: In the first stanza "act on things before they unfold" conveys a notable feature of early Chinese thinking. Existing things and the complexes we call "situations" possess an internal dynamic that shapes future development. In the shamanic tradition this dynamic was the basis for attempts to divine future outcomes by scrutinizing certain chance events. The Wisdom tradition dismissed such practices and emphasized instead the ability to influence incipient tendencies before lines of development have hardened their trajectory. The first stanza stresses the importance of early detection and intervention. Skill in this method uses the early flexibility of spontaneous activity to realize the Wisdom design of harmony and balance.

The second stanza adds to what was said on the topic of wise governance in DDJ 63. The last stanza speaks to the character, commitment, and self-discipline of those who follow the Way of the ancient Sages by assisting the self-ordering of the myriad things.*

65. Political Ecology II

The ancients who were good at
practicing the Way did not use it
to explain things to the populace,
but to lead them toward simplicity.

Governing is difficult when people
are overly clever. To use cleverness
to govern is to steal from the country.
And not to use cleverness to govern
a country is to benefit the country.
Understanding these two [precepts]
is also a check on one's design.
Always knowing how to check
one's design is profound attainment.

Profound attainment is deep and
far-reaching! It supports the return
of things thus one after another until
they reach the Great Succession.

Comment: In this verse the wisdom of guarding ecological balance is formulated as a political practice. Ancients who were adept at practicing the Way were known for using their profound attainment to preserve (DDJ 7) and to further life (DDJ 10), while protecting it from cultural designs (DDJ 29) and knowledge instruments (DDJ 18, 19, 41) that degrade life's holistic endowment and capacity for renewal.

The ancients are being presented as models of wise governance to political leaders at a time when the Zhou clan confederacy has collapsed and rulers of large states have begun employing clever knowledge specialists who discard holistic understanding and devise new stratagems for the centralization of power and control. Rulers who use these clever instruments are said to "steal from the country," because they add to the burden of excess design and control and thereby weaken the non-designed, self-organizing ecologies of society and nature.

The Wisdom tradition's "profound attainment" counters the pseudo-sage's partial conception of knowledge with the holistic understanding that sustainable harmony requires designs that preserve sufficiency and bring about the return of all things "one after the other" to the sustainable cycle of Being and Non-being.

The collective designs of human society have the potential to disrupt the balanced sufficiency stabilized by the cycle of return. Those who practice the Way help things "return" by intervening early to reverse unsustainable practices and "reconnect" the design thrust of collective human activity with the greater cyclical pattern of the Way, metaphorically referred to here as "the Great Succession."

66. Lesson in Governance V

Great rivers can be kings
of a hundred valley streams
because they are adept at
staying below them; this is
why they can be the kings
of a hundred valley streams.
Therefore, those who want
to be above the people, must
be humble in their speech
and subordinate their self-
interest to that of the people.

For this reason when the sages
hold high positions the people
are not burdened, and when
they hold leading positions
the people are not harmed.
This is why the world gladly
advances them and does not
tire of them. Since they do not
contend for power, no one in the
world can contend with them.

Comment: The verse continues the instruction of DDJ 60 and 61. The doctrine of non-contention voiced in the final line is found also DDJ 22, 68, 73 and in the final line of DDJ 81.

67. Wisdom's Three Treasures

*All the world says our Way greatly
resembles not much of anything.
But precisely because it is great
it seems like not much of anything.
If it resembled anything, it would
long ago have been a trifle!*

*We have three treasures that
we hold on to and preserve.
The first is called Caring.
The second is called Conservation.
The third is called Not Presuming
To Be First in the World.
With caring one can be bold.
With conservation one can be
expansive. By not presuming
to be the world's first, one can
become the senior over specialists.*

*Today [rulers] abandon caring
while being bold; abandon
conservation while expanding;
abandon humbling the self while
trying to be first—this is death!
For with caring one fights and
wins; in defense one stands firm.
When Heaven is going to save
those who fight, it is by means
of caring that they are protected.*

Comment: The Way is great even though it is small and unseen (DDJ 14), "without distinction" (DDJ 32), and what it effects "seems lacking" (DDJ 45). Calling it "great" provokes laugher from scholars of the lower ranks (DDJ 41), who fail to see its greatness is the constancy with which it supports everything else. If it were to resemble things that are commonly thought to be great it would lack this constancy because all such things are transitory processes. The second stanza gives the three "treasures" or leading values of the Wisdom tradition.

The final stanza is directed to a "present time" in which the Way has been lost and rulers are acting contrary to its wisdom. Since they have severed the lifeline of constancy and renewal, the text says their path leads to death. The final line offers a way out with the virtue of "caring" replacing the lost solidarity of kinship based on the blood ties of the ruling clans.*

68. Non-Contention

Those good at soldiering
are not militant.
Those adept at warfare
are not angry.
Those good at defeating enemies
do not engage them .
Those adept at utilizing people
subordinate [egoistic designs].
This is called the attainment of
non-contention. It means using
the strength of others. This is
called pairing with Heaven, the
highest principle of the ancients.

Comment: Non-contention is fundamental to the Wisdom of the Way. Contention occurs in speech (dispute and argument) and in action (acts that oppose, including acts of aggression and organized warfare). Examples in the first stanza show that the latter is the important category in this verse. DDJ 73 says that the Way of Heaven sustains without contention. In nature opposed tendencies undergo reversal and balanced sufficiency is restored without design and effort. Hence, there is no contention. With human societies this not the case. Contention arises from competing desires for power and control. The ancient sages therefore made non-contention the model for social and political decision-making, "using the strength of others" to attain by design the unity that obtains in nature without design. Non-contention within society enables humanity to unite its designs with the self-organizing processes of nature, thereby "obtaining the world" (DDJ 48, 57) by gaining the support of the world's most stable and productive activity. It is the consistent teaching of the ancient sages that this gain is defeated by contention for power and control.*

69. Moving Without Marching

[Regarding] the use of military force
it is said: "I dare not act as host,
but instead act as guest; dare not
advance an inch, but retreat a foot."
This is called moving without marching
rolling up one's sleeves without baring
one's arms, disposing of [enemies]
without hostilities, defeating them
without the force of arms.

There is no greater calamity
than underestimating the enemy.
If we take the enemy lightly
we lose our treasures. For when
opposing armies are evenly matched,
victory goes to those that grieve.

Comment: The Ho Shang Kung commentary says the guest "adapts himself and does not take the lead" (Erkes, p. 118). In Chinese martial arts using the strength of an opponent is a strategy for gaining the advantage. Retreating a foot rather than advancing an inch is called "moving without marching" because marching is taking the offensive with designing action, while moving in response is the flexible maneuver born of non-design. The flexible response overcomes the rigid design of the march. Defeating enemies without weapons may refer to the strategy of entrapping them.

70. Wisdom and Ignorance

My words are easy to understand
and easy to put into practice, but
the world is not able to understand
them or to put them into practice.

My words have a lineage,
My service has a sovereign.
Because the world is ignorant
[of these] I am not known.

Those who know me are few.
Those following me are valued.
This is why sages wear coarse
cloth and carry jade within.

Comment: In this verse the speaker seems to be an adept of the Way whose followers are few and whose efforts to transmit the ancient holistic wisdom have failed, even though his words are easy to understand and to practice. But if the speaker's teachings are easy to understand, why haven't they been understood by ruling elites? The 2nd stanza says the answer has to do with ignorance of the Wisdom tradition and the Constant Way that is "the sovereign" of its teachings. The next verse, which may have originally formed a unit with this one, relates such ignorance to the pathology of power.*

71. A Disease of Ignorance

To understand ignorance
is a higher [attainment].
Ignorance of understanding
is an illness.

Only when this illness
is understood to be an illness
is it no longer an illness.

People of wisdom do not
suffer from this illness.
Because they understand
it to be an illness,
they are free of it.

Comment: The original core of the ancient sages' Wisdom of the Way is seen in their teaching that the basis of the world's constancy and sustainability is not to be found in the power of human designs to *dominate,* but in the much greater "power" of non-designed activity to *sustain.* The previous verse states that ignorance is the reason this teaching has not been understood and acted on. This verse adds that ignorance of this sort is an illness. Not all ignorance is said to be pathological, only the type that was parodied in DDJ 41, where those who are literate and have cultivated abilities are shown to be unable to grasp what simple people living in sustainable communities have long understood.

In traditional Chinese medicine healthy well-being is the normal condition of a balanced sufficiency in which there is neither deficiency nor excess (DDJ 3).

Illness is understood as a disharmony of functions that are normally "in balance" (Kapchuck, chap. 1). Sickness in the individual, or in the body of society as a whole, is thus a sign of disharmony in the sustaining unity of the supportive processes of life

Ignorance of understanding is a sickness in this sense. Since opposites are said to arise together (DDJ 2), the insufficiency the Wisdom tradition traces here to an ignorance of understanding is linked to the types of excess described in verses 9, 12, 13, 24, 30, 44, 46, 53, 72, 74 and 75. The disordering effects of excess on human personality go a long way toward explaining how it is that words said to be easy to understand and easy to put practice could be incomprehensible to those in positions of authority in the hierarchy of power.*

72. Lesson in Governance VI

When commoners do not fear terror,
then a greater terror has arrived.

Do not infringe on their settlements.
Do not abhor their manner of living.
It is because you do not revile them
that they have no loathing of you.

People of wisdom know themselves
and do not make a display themselves;
they care for themselves and do not
elevate themselves. Thus they leave
the latter and choose the former.

Comment: The Wisdom tradition's political ecology aims at dissuading rulers from the use of force. The opening lines are a warning to rulers about the limits to the use of force. DDJ 74 says a line is crossed when a people no longer fear death. When this happens a force greater than a ruler can control has arrived. Wang Bi's comment is: "When the common people are unable to bear the weight of this power any longer, they burst forth in a flood from top to bottom" (Lynn/WB 180).

73. The Net of Heaven

Those with the bravery to defy death
are slain. Those whose bravery does
not defy death live. Of these two, either
may bring benefit or harm. Who knows
why Heaven hates what it does?

The Way of Heaven does not contend
but is good at sustaining; does not speak
but responds well; does not summon
but things come on their own; makes no
effort [at design] but counsels well.

Heaven's net is vast and wide-spaced
but it allows nothing to slip through.

Comment: The first stanza speaks to the difficulty in understanding the "why" of events which originate in spontaneous changes rather than in design. Despite this element of uncertainty the second stanza confirms the overall beneficial workings of natural processes. The final couplet then presents the deeper layer of meaning in the Wisdom tradition's holistic teaching of the overall beneficial outcome of non-designed activity. The world's constancy is contingent on each thing's returning to its origin in Non-being. Heaven's net is is open to evolving changes, but nothing escapes the pattern of return.

74. On The Death Penalty

If people do not fear death,
how can anyone use death to
cowl them? If people always
caused to fear death make
trouble, and I seize them and
kill them, who then would dare?
The Great Executioner is always
there to do the killing. To take
over for the Great Executioner
who does the killing is like
standing in to hew [wood] for
the master craftsman. Of those
who do so, there are few that
do not injure their hands.

Comment: If people do not fear death, then the threat of capital punishment is useless. If, however, they value their lives the threat of death acts as an effective deterrent. But if rulers themselves become executioners by acting in place of the "Great Executioner" (natural death), they are unlikely to escape without injury.

75. Starvation, Taxes and Death

*People starve because the ruling elites
take too much in tax-grain--this is why
they starve. People are hard to govern
because the ruling elites have designs
on the world—this is why they are hard
to govern. People have little concern
for death because the ruling elites seek
life's fullness [for themselves]. This is
why they take death lightly. Only those
who do not use life as a means are able
to value life.*

Comment: The verse repeats the Wisdom tradition's theme that excesses on
the part of the ruling elites are disruptive of balanced sufficiency and social
harmony. The message of the final sentence presses home the holistic idea
that the life-world is a "sacred vessel" that cannot be made an object of design.
To use it as a means to an end is "to ruin it" (DDJ 29). Thus, those who *do not*
seek to subordinate life's holistic order to aggrandizing designs are said to be
able to value life in the sense of caring for the integrity and well-being of the
entire life-community.

76. Attributes of Life and Death

In life people are supple and yielding.
In death they are stiff and unyielding.
The myriad things, like grasses and
trees, are in life supple and crisp; in
death they are withered and sere. Thus,
the stiff and unyielding attends death;
the supple and yielding attends life.

This is why unyielding armies do not
win, and unbending trees snap in two.
The stiff and unyielding dwell below.
The supple and yielding dwell above.

Comment: What is supple and yielding appears weak but has more constancy. What is firm and unyielding projects strength but has less "staying power." The teaching of the Wisdom tradition is that constancy comes from staying close to the Way. Reversing the Way's pattern of constancy by relying on the unyielding strength of resistance will weaken sustainability.

77. The Way of Heaven

Isn't The Way of Heaven
like the drawing of a bow!
What is higher is lowered,
What is lower is pulled up.
If [the tension] is excessive
reduce it. If it is insufficient
supply it [by tightening].

The Way of Heaven
reduces excess and
supplements deficiency
The Way of Men is different.
It takes from deficiency
to supplement excess.

Who can have a surplus
and offer it to the world ?
Only those having the Way.
This is why sages act but
do not depend [on design];
they accomplish works of
merit but do not dwell [on
them]; they have no desire
to display their ability.

Comment: In the ancient Wisdom of the Way constancy and stability in the natural world are the result of a dynamic equilibrium that is protected against runaway divergent processes by a limiting corrective function called the Way of Heaven. The commonplace action of testing a bow is used to illustrate the Way of Heaven's innate tendency based on a naturally functioning *principle of sufficiency*. A bow requires sufficient tension in the bowstring to launch arrows. Too little tension and the arrows will not fly, too much and the bowstring cannot be pulled. Analogously, life requires a relative balance of stable conditions to flourish and reproduce. The Way of Heaven is a set phrase for the tendency in nature that restores balance by reducing excess and supplementing deficiency. This natural sufficiency function is absent from "the Way of Men." In its place the Wisdom tradition finds harmful human designs that compound excess by exploiting the needy. Relevant examples occur in DDJ 53 and 75. People of wisdom do not hoard (DDJ 81), but offer their surplus to the world because their counter-design is holistic, rather than egoistic. Their goal is not to amass benefits for themselves, but to see that the flow of natural abundance is not blocked and the sufficiency of the life network is not ruined by human designs that seek to dominate natural processes.*

78. Lesson in Governance VII

Nothing in the world is as pliant
or weak as water. Yet for attacking
what is firm and strong, nothing
can surpass it. For this reason
there is nothing to take its place.
The weak wins out over the strong.
the pliant wins out over the firm.
Though no one in the world is
unacquainted [with this proverb],
none is able to put it into practice.

Therefore, the ancient sages said:
To accept the country's dirt is to be
Lord of the Altars of Soil and Grain.
To bear the country's misfortunes
is to be king of all under Heaven.
True words seem like the opposite.

Comment: The first stanza adds to what is said about water in DDJ 8 by linking it to the doctrine that the Way's greatness is such that even though it appears weak and pliant nothing can subjugate it (DDJ 32). The verse's lesson in governance continues the large state-small state discussions of DDJ 61 and 62.*

79. Reconciliation

In reconciling great grievances
some ill will is bound to remain.
How can this [lingering ill will]
be remedied? By responding to
it with [Wisdom's] attainment.
Therefore, people of wisdom hold
to [their part of] the contract and
make no demands on the other.
Those with attainment attend
to the agreement. Those lacking
attainment attend to the payment.

The Way of Heaven is impartial;
it constantly supports those who
are good [at practicing the Way].

Comment: Practicing the wisdom of the Way presupposes a "higher attainment" (DDJ 38), illustrated in this verse by the handling of disputes about contractual agreements. Those who practice the Way understand the greater good of preserving or recovering harmony, and they therefore respond with tolerance (DDJ 16) rather than with the application of force. In the closing lines the impartiality shown by those practicing the Way coincides with and therefore gains the support of Heaven's greater pattern of balance.*

80. A Vision of Permaculture

Envision a world of small states
with limited populations. If labor-
saving implements existed they
would not be in use, and if people
took death seriously they would not
travel far. Even though they had
boats and carriages no one would
ride in them, and even though they
had armor and weapons, they would
not be [routinely] displayed.

[Moreover] if the people had gone
back to using knotted cords, their
foods were sweet, their clothing
attractive, their homes tranquil
and secure, and their customs full
of joy, then even if neighboring
countries overlooked one another
and the people could hear each
other's roosters and dogs, they
would grow old and die without
comings and goings between them.

Comment: The verse suggests that sustainable communities develop naturally
without ruling elites telling them what to do. We see the "lighter footprint"
of smaller populations. The valuing of life ("taking death seriously") requires
that the resilience of natural systems be protected.

The reason the populations of these small countries are said not to travel far, even though they have boats and carriages, is given in the second stanza: their way of life is one of cultivated sufficiency. Living on the land and not migrating are therefore the twin themes that hold the verse together.

The second stanza goes deeper into the issue of technology, suggesting that whereas an adequate material culture (food, clothing, and housing) and a fulfilling tradition of customs and beliefs are essential, writing and literacy are not. Their absence from an idealized sketch of a sustainable way of life is therefore significant. None of the features of culture mentioned requires the intervention of class of literate specialists "to see to it" that they are part of the life of the country, and no mention is made of the class of "scholarly officials" who assist the rulers of states.

The verse also weighs against the traditional "Taoist" interpretation, which says that the *Dao De Jing* advocates *wuwei*—a life without conscious design activity. Even the simple agrarian way of life depicted here has cultural aspects that require purposeful design decision-making in order to secure material sufficiency and a satisfying cultural tradition.*

81. The Way of the Sages

Words of trust are not artful.
Artful speech is not trustworthy.
Those adept [at the Way] do
not dispute. Those who dispute
are not adept [at the Way].
Those who understand are
not learned. The learned do
not understand.

Sages do not hoard.
Since they act for others,
they themselves have more.
By giving support to others,
they better their own store.
The Way of Heaven is to
benefit without cutting.
The Way of the Sages is
to act without contending.

Comment: The verse begins with the cultural obstacles to enlightenment: artful rather than plain speech, verbal contention rather than holistic understanding, and the sort of learning that is condemned as a waste in DDJ 20. The second stanza then addresses the psychological and economic obstacle to practicing the Way—the tendency to hoard. Hoarding disrupts sustainable harmony (DDJ 42) by "excessive storing" (DDJ 44), which "brings on the burden of loss." This is why those following the Way do not hoard, and do not desire excess (DDJ 15). They understand that disaccumulation remedies the imbalance caused by hoarding. Accumulating beyond general sufficiency brings deficits, because opposites arise together (DDJ 2). Wisdom adepts recognize that reversing imbalance protects the general store, which results in their "having more." This "more" is not an excess accumulation on their part, but consists in betterment of the general health of the commons, the supportive order whose productivity the Way of the Sages is designed to assist (DDJ 64), "preserve" (DDJ 7, 28), "care for" (DDJ 13), become "one with" (DDJ 16, 22, 23, 39, 56, 68), "enhance" (DDJ 51), "safeguard" (DDJ 52), "look after" (DDJ 59), "honor" and "treasure" (DDJ 20 and 62), "support" (DDJ 64 and 65), "cultivate" (DDJ 54) and "make a contribution to" (DDJ 9). The design in the actions of those who follow this Way replaces the contentious egoism of accumulationist designs with acts that neither "take possession," "dominate" nor "lay claim to" (DDJ 2, 10, 51). They are therefore able to "get beyond the self" (DDJ 7) and preserve life by attaining to the oneness called for by holistic understanding.*

ADDITIONAL COMMENTS

1. The Constant Way

Heaven [tian1] and Earth [di4] comprise the universe of Being [you3], also called "the One" (DDJ 39). Therefore, the verse is consistent with DDJ 40 which says that Being is born of Non-being [wu2]. The latter is the aspect of the total universe that is inscrutable because it is beyond our power of examination (DDJ 14). It is therefore called "profoundly mysterious." This may be the intent of the opening line, which says the Constant Way [chang2 dao4] is a Way that cannot be spoken about or explained.

2. The Unity of Opposites

The traditional "Taoist" reading of wu2 wei2 is "without action." It gave rise to the mystical idea that sage-kings are able to manage their domains without doing anything. This idea makes it hard if not impossible to understand the wisdom of balancing opposites, since no "opposite" independent of all human management is recognized. The independent opposite dimension, natural activity, is the subject of the 2nd stanza. Sages of the ancient Wisdom tradition directed attention to this dimension when rulers attempted to subject the entire world [tian1 xia4] to their designs (DDJ 29). The sages did this in order to emphasize the fact that the natural dimension of the world already has a stable and continuing non-designed order and that human communities ignoring this fact run the risk of weakening the constancy of the very processes they are dependent on.

3. Wisdom's Supportive Order

In the verse's final line the set phrase wei2 wu 2 wei2 encapsulates the teaching of the ancient "way of the sages" (DDJ 81). Read literally it appears to be a paradoxical instruction to "act without action." But wei2 means instrumental action designed to obtain a certain result, and it is just this aspect of action that is being negated by the expression wu2 wei2. Like Being and Non-being, wei2 and wu2 wei2 are polar opposites that "arise together." Wu2 wei2 does not mean the absence of all activity (since that would mean that nature, which is without design, is also be without activity). In the wei2 wu2 wei2 maxim the ancient sages were drawing attention to the importance of natural activity as the opposite of human design activity and as the dimension in which the effects of human action register and have an impact. The purpose of the wei2 wu2 wei2 maxim, therefore, is to communicate a "way" [dao4] that enables humanity to accomplish by design the same balancing and unification of opposites that occurs spontaneously in nature, a process which DDJ 77 calls "the Dao of Heaven" [tian1 zhi1 dao4].

5. Impartiality and Impermanence

The first line says Heaven and Earth are bu4 ren2, often translated as "not humane," or "not benevolent." "Humane" is the post-Confucian meaning of ren2. Brooks and Brooks note that before Confucius, ren2 defined "the traits of an ideal comrade-at-arms" (p. 15). Graham says ren2 was the word "the aristocratic clans of the Zhou used to distinguish themselves from the common people" (p. 19). The aristocratic clans based their identity on common descent and were discriminatory on that basis. In saying that Heaven and Earth are not "ren2," therefore, the ancient sages meant that the cosmos is impartial with regard to descent. This is consistent with DDJ 79, which says the Way of Heaven does not discriminate on the basis of kin relationship.

Thus, Heaven and Earth do not play favorites, and this is what we expect in a naturalistic world-view. DDJ 56 confirms this view when it says "There is no being closely or distantly related to [the Way]."

In the first stanza the "straw dogs" metaphor introduces the principle of universal impermanence and then applies it to the ancient ruling clans, the bai3 xing4, in order to demystify and debunk their claim to ruling power derived from an immortal ancestor. In place of the ruling clan idea of de2, meaning "virtue" in the sense of an inherited power, the ancient sages taught that virtue [de2] is an attainment that does not risk ruining the stability and balance of the life-world by trying to dominate it (DDJ 29). The second stanza is related to the first by way of contrast. The contrast, made explicit in DDJ 77, is that between the Way of Heaven and the Way of Men, and specifically, between the sufficiency and balance of the former and the excess and deficiency of the latter. In this verse the Way of Heaven is depicted as a bellows that does not fail to supply more. This contrasts with the power apparatus of the ruling clans, whose tax policies result in an enervating reversal, a "caving in" or collapse into insufficiency and want (see the examples in DDJ 75 and 77).

7. Reversal of Egoism

The second stanza contains a subtle play on the word shen1, which means both the self as a psycho-social body and the self as an organic body, the natural organism that is part of the life network. The ancient sages were holistic in their wisdom and cultivated the attainment of a virtue that enabled them to step away from the demands of the ego-driven self in order to give conscious attention and care to preserving the organic body of life as a whole, on which they and the human community of individual beings are dependent. The rhetorical question at the end of the verse suggests that by a reversal of egoism the sages were able to complete their personal aim of "higher attainment" (DDJ 38). The mystical "Taoist" version of the final line advances the idea that by giving up private interests they were able to realize those interests, so that the very goals abandoned could be attained. With ego-self and bodily-self distinguished, this paradoxical reading is avoided.

10. Profound Attainment
The "four" [si4] are cast in the form of maxims, rather than as the factual descriptions of DDJ 2. The main variation between the two sets is the addition of the fourth maxim: to promote or further without domination [chang2 er2 bu4 zai3]. The "four" serve as a paradigm for the attainment that the final line calls xuan2 de2, meaning "dark, or profound virtue." De2 ("virtue") is also translated as "power" (Waley) , "efficacy" (Ames and Hall) and as "integrity" (Mair) . Chang translated de2 as "attainment." In the Additional Comments to DDJ 38 I have examined the problem involved in rendering the concept of de2 in English.

13. Valuing Life Above Rank
On the ecological ordering of values, see for example the works by Callicott, Ereira, and Waters. Concerning China's ancient feudal clan-based civilization, anthropologists refer to institutional power of this type as the "tribal-consanguineal state" (Krader, pp 4-5), because ties of kinship and ancestral lineage play a fundamental role its continuity. Ruling power of this sort creates a peculiar set of stresses arising from competition for rank and rulership. See Elias' comments on "this compelling struggle for ever-threatened power and prestige..." (p. 87).

15. Ancient Adepts of the Way

Concerning the concluding line of this verse, Lynn writes (p. 75) that, "Throughout the ages, most commentators have rejected Wang Bi's interpretation" and followed instead "the much more common textual variant," found for example in the Fu Yi text. The Wang Bi text is "Since there is no excess, therefore neng2 bi4, meaning "can be sheltered, covered or concealed." The Fu Yi text has neng2 and bi4 (without the grass radical), which means "can be worn out, ragged, or damaged." DDJ 21 and 22 confirm the teaching that the Way's continuity gives assurance that *in the holistic sense* ruin can be accompanied by renewal.

The Quietist reading found in most popular presentations of "Taoism" assumes the Wisdom response is passive and acquiescent, and in this verse that the answer to the rhetorical "who" questions is "no one." There is ample recognition in the *Dao De Jing*, however, that cultural designs mediate the human response to nature and that a "wuwei culture" is not a possibility. The cultural attainments mentioned in DDJ 80 serve as an obvious example of the mediating work of human design.

16. The Meaning of Constancy

The problem of constancy, continuance, stability and sustainability is central to the teachings of the ancient wisdom tradition (or "Way of the Sages" DDJ 81), and is evidence of the ecological theme in the *Dao De Jing*. In nature, constancy is sustained by a "return" that limits extreme tendencies by "reversing" them (DDJ 77). Reversal accomplishes a return from Being to Non-being, defined as the opposite of "being things." In the life-world this process supports a continuing fertility sufficient for life to flourish. In DDJ 55, chang2 is used in a similar sentence conjoined with the word he2, meaning harmony: "To know harmony is called constancy." This definition brings us close to the contemporary meaning of homeostasis, a key feature of sustainability in the life environment. Claude Bernard, the 19th century father of physiology, developed the idea of constancy within the body, which Walter Cannon in *The Wisdom of the Body*, renamed homeostasis and applied to both inner and outer constancy. Cannon's homeostasis requires cooperating functions and "actions" that maintain the constancy of the environment.

17. Ruling Power and the Decline of Trust

The traditional interpretation of the opening line of this verse is the one found in the Ho Shang Kung commentary: "By highest antiquity the nameless princes of the highest antiquity are meant" (Erkes, p. 39). Not only is this view at odds with the text (there is no word for ruler or "princes" and the subject of the sentence is left vague), it misrepresents the nature of the early societies, which were without the institution of rulership. In the second stanza we see a resort to the swearing of oaths, a situation that was part of the collapse of the consanguineal state and its replacement over time by the family-based dynastic system of the imperial state (see Eberhard's account of ancient China's transition from clan-based feudalism to a gentry-elite state system in his *A History of China*, chaps. 2-6). A later chapter of the *Zhuangzi* says, "The greatest trust is shown in not swearing oaths (23.11, Legge II, p. 87).

18. When the Great Way Was Abandoned

The path of decline from trust to distrust is repeated in this verse, which opens with the suggestion that Confucian teachings are a symptom of the decline that occurs "when the Way is lost" (DDJ 38). Both the *Dao De Jing* and the *Zhuangzi* show unrelenting opposition to the artificial, conformist monoculture of vertical civilizations designed to idealize, standardize and enshrine forms that are "sublimely" without flaw. These ideals are seen as creating deficiencies where none exist, then promoting capable specialists to "give things" their "correct form" (*Zhuangzi* 8.2, Legge I, p. 271), a practice that "distorts and vexes the world" *(ibid.)*.

20. A Wisdom Adept in the Courtly Crowd

Ancient Chinese court society was highly regulated, even to the point of prescribing certain postures and facial expressions for different formal occasions. (Dobson, p. 193). A feature of the tai4 lao2, the "Feast of the Great Sacrifice," was the opportunity to indulge in three kinds of meat: beef, mutton, and pork. In the second stanza the word *zhao4,* translated here as "sign," can also mean "omen." Since the Wisdom tradition dismisses divination as a frivolous pastime (DDJ 38), the "sign" here may point inward to a state of mind.

21. The Way and Its Continuity

The opening line of this verse can be read in two ways, depending on whether *de2* (most often translated as "virtue") means virtue *attained*, or virtue as inborn *endowment.* The Wisdom tradition saw virtue in new-born infants as a natural endowment (DDJ 55) which is diminished in adults, who are said to be fond of bypaths (DDJ 53). It is a *"great attainment"* for an adult to be able to do what new-borns do naturally— namely, to just go along with the Way.

22. Wisdom Embraces Oneness

"Bent yet whole" [qu1 ze2 quan2] has a variety of translations, but they are alike in making the sage the subject and giving the verse an anthropocentric reading. Lin Yutang, for example, reads the opening line as "To yield is to be preserved whole." Ch'u Ta-Kao's translation is "Be humble, and you will remain entire." The problem is that what applies to the whole does not necessarily transfer to the parts. The Constant Way (which includes the whole of Being and Non-being) is a process of wearing away accompanied by constant renewal. Being as a whole is renewed, but only because the individual beings that comprise Being at any given moment are "bent" toward their return to Non-being. As a result the cycle of the whole continues. The ancient sages embraced oneness or wholeness (were holistic in their thinking and in their practical adaptation to conditions) because the holistic path (dao4 or method) does not degrade the constancy and continuity of earthly Being. In strengthening constancy they support the life environment as a whole. Although this may contribute to their own longevity, it does not mean that *they* will be preserved whole and constantly renewed (i.e. become immortal).

25. The Great Way

The *Dao De Jing* does not say whether humanity once spontaneously followed the Great Way, but it is clear that it makes a case for saying that the collective design of the emerging vertical civilization no longer conforms to the fa3, the law, of the great pattern that ensures constancy or sustainability. Graham writes that the core doctrine of the *Dao De Jing* and the *Zhuangzi* is "that while other things move spontaneously on the course proper to them, man has separated himself from the Way by reflecting, posing alternatives, and formulating principles of action" (p. 172). If, like Heaven/Earth (Nature), the fa3 of humanity were naturally and spontaneously aligned with the constant cycle of the Great Way, the teachings of the *Dao De Jing* would be ornamental rather than practical and ecologically compelling, and their transmission would be pointless.

26. Two Practical Maxims

In the practical logic of naturalistic thinking, natural processes (spontaneous and without design) are "weightier" or have greater importance than the designing actions of human beings by reason of the fact that they have greater stability and constancy. The lesser stability and constancy of human designs is evident in the fact that they depend on additional complex mental processes run through the loop of consciousness. Self-organizing processes take place without dependence on design and control by conscious decision making.

27. Transmission of the Light

In the pedagogical context of this chapter xi2 ming2 translates as "carrying on or following the pattern of the light." Since xi2 also has the meaning of "double" or "two-fold" Duyvendak rendered xi2 ming2 as "a twofold understanding." Ch'u Ta-kao treats it as "double enlightenment." In this case transmission of the light from teacher to student would be understood as "enlightenment doubled."

29. The Failure of Imperial Design

Hsueh Hui's definition of excess has deep roots in prehistory (See, for example, Sahlins, chap. 1). Because prehistoric, so-called "primitive," civilizations lacked the technology, vertical order and "armies of labor" to make and sustain large-scale modifications of the environment, they were of necessity more attuned to the need for adaptive designs that preserved ecological balance. The ecological wisdom transmitted in the *Dao De Jing* carries forward this pre-historic "attunement" and insight regarding the cost in terms energy and labor time of increasing cultural complexity and economic domination.

To act "on the world" [tian1 xia4] is to seek to modify it by design. In the *Dao De Jing* this set expression is used naturalistically to mean the whole earth environment. In legendary and mythic writing this corresponds to the holistic notion of a "kingdom" or "realm," and is best translated as "the world." Human designs alter the natural ecologies of the world in ways that can be sustained only with continued expenditure of energy. Calling the world a "sacred" or "divine" vessel [shen1 qi4] is meant to introduce the counter-idea that it is not just an expanse terri-tory for conquest and domination. The meaning of shen1 qi4 is metaphorical and derives from the tripod urn used in religious sacrifices. Although the vessel was a product of craft design it obtained a sacred aura by virtue of its use in communicat-ing with the dead. In treating this religious object symbolically the ancient wisdom tradition sought to convey the non-cultural, "divine" character of the world-totality, which exhibits great constancy and continuous production without effort.

31. Weapons

On the "culture of militarism," see Vagts, chap. 1. This is one of the verses of the Wang Bi text that lacks a commentary and scholars have suggested his comments may have become mixed up with what is identified as the text. What is omitted from the present translation are details about the behavior of feudal lords in times of peace and war (e.g. in prosperous times it is said that the ruling lord "gives preference the left, in difficult times pref-erence shifts to the right"). Duyvenak notes that the suggestion has been made "that the entire text is nothing but a commentary on the previous [verse]" (p. 78).

32. The Way Is Without Name and Rank

"The Way is without name and rank" translates dao4 chang2 wu2 ming2. Ming2 means name, but also fame, reputation and rank in feudal society. Clarity requires the inclusion of "rank" as well as "name" in the translation, because the sentence goes on to add that the Way is "small" (has no social standing) and yet nothing in the world, including the political power structure, can rule over it. This is the understanding of ming2 we find in the Wang Bi commentary. The second stanza says that if the kings and nobles guard the Way, then the myriad beings will zi4 bin1. This expression has several possible meanings. Some English translations have the myriad beings "submitting" (Chan, Hendricks, Lau) or "deferring" (Ivanhoe, Ames & Hall) to the nobles and kings. Others have them becoming "guests" (Lin, Roberts, Chen and Wilhelm) of the nobles and kings. Bronze Age inscriptions show bin1 also has the meaning of "gift," as in "to present a gift" (Schuessler, p. 167), so that another interpretation of zi4 bin1 would have the myriad beings spontaneously giving and the princes and kings benefiting from the productive abundance that flows from a healthy life environment.

The third stanza speaks to the problem of the expansion of "names and ranks," that is, the growth of the elite class that lives from tribute rather than labor. The hereditary feudal system put in place by the Zhou clan confederacy was much like the one that appeared in Europe following the disintegration of the Roman Empire. Even the titles of the various ranks correspond (Hsu, p. 5). The expansion of these ranks began as early as the initial conquest of the Shang (1122 BCE). Since the leaders of the Shang also ruled over a hereditary feudal system, the elites of the conquering Zhou people took over, by a process of "super-stratification," an already stratified society (Eberhard, p. 24). The growth of elite ranks continued thereafter by the practice of "subinfeudation," a process whereby the offspring of ruling elites were also enfeoffed, that is, given control of productive land and labor sufficient to maintain their standing (Hsu, p. 8). Obviously, without expansion of the agricultural base the system grows top-heavy and unstable, as more and more tributary product must be extracted from the primary producers of wealth in the system. "Stopping," therefore, implies either stopping the practice of enfeoffing offspring, or something more radical, such as leveling the entire system.

36. The Problem of Transmission

There is wide disagreement among commentators on the meaning of this verse. A common misunderstanding, dating back to Han Fei and the "Legalists," is that the four maxims are "techniques" of political stagecraft for getting an opponent to destroy himself. The fourth maxim, however, does not fit this interpretation. The idea, for example, of *giving* power to someone (with the express intention of recovering it for oneself) is more likely to produce an outcome like that experienced by Prospero in the *The Tempest*. This suggests that the maxims are not meant as techniques of self-aggrandizement, but as examples of the "subtle understanding" of the unity and balance of opposites, which when disturbed by an extreme tendency will eventually re-establish itself by reversing that tendency (DDJ 77). It is in this context that the adaptability of what is flexible and weak wins out over the firm and strong. Since the former does not "force the beam" (DDJ 42), it is able to maintain balance and continue when the extreme tendency suffers reversal. This "subtle understanding" is also what is meant by saying that "the Great Way is very level and safe but people prefer bypaths" (DDJ 53). The "Fish" analogy that closes the verse will not then mean concealing a country's "sharp weapons," the most common translation of li4 qi4. In this context the more likely meaning of this expression is "beneficial asset," which both fits as a description of the "subtle understanding" and serves an explanation of the fish analogy. Just as fish do not survive being separated from their natural habitat, the subtle understanding of how the Way functions doesn't survive outside the "natural habitat" of the inner training required for enlightenment about the true source of constancy.

37. Self-Organization and Desire

In the opening sentence wu2 wei2 is paradoxically conjoined with the double negative wu2 bu4 wei2, usually translated as "nothing not done." While this is a possible translation it is not successful because it leaves open the possibility that the Way is involved in action, in doing things. Action implies purposeful doing in association with conscious design, which the first part of the opening sentence, dao4 chang2 wu2 wei2, explicitly rules out. The non-paradoxical point being made is that the Way is not responsible for the formation of order in the world; stable order arises in the absence of the activity of design or a designer. The expression "order for free" is borrowed from Stuart Kauffman's study of biological complexity, emergent order and self-organization.

The wisdom transmitted in the *Dao De Jing* does not develop a distinction between wants (desires) and needs. Most likely this is not an unintended omission. In so-called "primitive" civilizations needs are defined by a principle of sufficiency that embodies a generally-recognized minimum necessary for life (Radin, pp 105-136, and Sahlins, chap. 5). In the *Dao De Jing* this minimum is recognized in the expression "what is enough" (DDJ 46). Desires can then be defined as motivating acquisitions in excess of this generally-recognized minimum. The vague assertion that "*we*" will "*moderate them*" using the simplicity of those without name or rank can be understood as a remedial response to stir those who live in simplicity to actions that restore stability and balance based on sufficiency.

38. Higher Attainment

The opening sentence is paradoxical; the literal meaning of shang4 de2 bu4 de2 is "Higher de2 is not de2." Translators usually add words not in the text to avoid the paradox of the literal;

e.g., "Superior Virtue *never assets* its virtue" (Duyvendak), or "The superior virtue is not *conscious of itself as* virtue" (Ch'u Ta-kao). Waley translated de2 as "power" instead of "virtue" and argued that de2 in the *Dao De Jing* has a "pre-moral" meaning "bound up with the idea of potentiality" (p. 32). The switch to "power" as the meaning of de2 is, however, unnecessary. The English word "virtue" originally had and still retains the "premoral" sense of "the beneficial quality or power of a thing" deriving from the old Latin root *virtus*, meaning an endowed strength, power or manliness. Christianity overlaid this ancient sense of "virtue" with a moral meaning that goes beyond the original endowment of strength or power. Christian virtue adds the quality of merit, which must be attained through adherence to a moral standard. Virtue then becomes an excellence that is *attained*. By switching to "power" as the translation of de2 Waley lost the sense of attainment that is part of the meaning of de2. In the *Dao De Jing,* de2 has both the meaning of an endowed potency (DDJ 55) and that of a cultivated attainment (DDJ 10), and both are necessary to resolve the paradox of the opening sentence of this verse. The two senses of "virtue," must be distinguished in contexts that would otherwise be ambiguous. The opening sentence, then, says that the de2 (virtue) of "higher attainment" does not increase one's de2 (virtue) of power or potency. What is cultivated in the de2 of higher attainment is *the protection* of the de2 of natural endowment. The *Zhuangzi* (5.1, Legge, p. 225) characterizes this sense of de2 as "the cultivation of a complete harmony." It is therefore not the attainment of something more pursued by a "lesser attainment" that seeks to enhance its potency by making gains through designing actions. The two senses of de2 are part of a coherent teaching that says the cultivation of higher attainment is the preservation of a harmony, not the acquisition of a personal gain. What is preserved by this attainment is the richness of the world's natural endowment.

42. Sustainable Harmony

The harmony from fusing vital breaths can mean harmony *within* the individual, harmony *among* a community of beings, or both. In the individual, harmony results presumably from self-cultivation. Wang Bi treated the fusion of vital breaths in a proto-ecological manner as harmony *among a community of beings*: "Although they have a myriad of forms, the fusion of vital breaths makes One out of them" (Lynn/Wang Bi, p. 135). In his *Fundamentals of Ecology* Odum writes that "In the ecosystem," the unified order of a bio-mass structure "is maintained by the total community respiration" which continually "pumps out" disorder (p. 37).

44. The Freedom of Sufficiency

"Debilitating" translates the word *bing4*, whose basic meaning is "sickness." Here *bing4* also has the sense of a mental "disorder" as well (as it does in DDJ 71).

48. Obtaining the World

For the problem with the traditional reading of wu2 wei2 er2 wu2 bu4 wei2 see the Additional Comment to DDJ 37 above. In DDJ 37 the topic is the Way. Here practitioners of the Way are instructed to model the Way by cutting back on designing action until they are "without any action of design," the point at which they will have "joined" with the Great Way of Constancy. The second stanza appears to instruct those following the Way to do what DDJ 29 says cannot be done without ruin—namely, qu3 tian1 xia4, "*to obtain the world*." Read ecologically and holistically, however, we see that in this verse, as in DDJ 57, obtaining the world is premised on the Wisdom tradition's enlightened understanding that the constancy of the world's natural processes is degraded by the effort to dominate them. This is why DDJ 46 says "There is no fault greater than desiring gain." The meaning of the expression *"obtain the world"* in the Wisdom tradition is not to take possession of and exert dominance over the world, but to benefit from the natural endowment of abundance that is already at hand as a result of its natural (non-designed) production. One *"obtains"* the world then by protecting the constancy of natural processes that, in "running on their own," provide the world's net primary production, the basis for whatever additional abundance human designs are able to develop.

49. Sages Are Impartial
The traditional reading of the first line of this verse is that the sages have no xin1, no heart/mind (ideas, sentiments, intentions) of their own, but take or regard the heart/mind of the "people," the bai3 xing4, as their own. This interpretation is inconsistent with the Wisdom tradition teaching that "complete stillness" is necessary for the "higher attainment" (DDJ 38) separating the sage from the pseudo-sage, an attainment whose holistic design is to conserve and "further" the natural endowment of the life community. Furthermore, in the historical context of the feudal consanguineal state, the expression bai3 xing4 does not mean "the people" but the "hundred clan-names" that refer to the members of the ruling class. The term came to refer to people in general only after the collapse of the consanguineal state and its replacement by the dynastic system which made all people (even the former nobility) mere subjects of the emperor. The reading offered here sees the verse as a lesson in contrast that teaches reversal of the psychology of elitism as essential for the preservation or recovery of peace, harmony and constancy based on sufficiency.

51. The Way Gives Life
In their *Ecological Design*, Van de Ryn and Cowan develop the idea of "bioremediation" to "gently catalyze" the potentialities

of nature (p. 130), and state that "Weaving nature back into everyday life breaks down destructive dichotomies between the built world and wild nature" (p. 163).

52. Safeguarding the Mother
The Fu Yi text has xi2 chang2 as in the final line, with the connotation of adapting and following an old practice. The holistic interpretation finds support throughout the *Dao De Jing*, especially in DDJ 54, where the transgenerational, multi-leveled concern for life is given a concise poetic expression.

54. Transgenerational Continuity
A well-established Wisdom practice binds past, present and future together in a transgenerational continuity that gives concrete meaning to the notion of constancy (sustainability). Constancy is conceived dynamically as the persistence of a tendency whose "homeostasis" (the Wisdom tradition's balance of sufficiency) ensures persistence "over a wider range of perturbations and further into the future..." (Turner, p. 219). Regarding ancestral worship, Sung Ch'ang-Hsing wrote: "In ancient times, ancestral worship consisted in...venerating ancestors as if they were present, and in thanking them for their virtuous example. Those who cultivate the Way likewise enable later generations to enjoy the fruits of their cultivations" (quoted in Red Pine, p. 108).

55. Natural Endowment in Its Fullness
Naturally endowed potency, de2, can be described as the "result" of the Way in the distinct and durable processes called "things." In this sense de2 is "that which obtains" (Mote, pp 76-77). Wagner translates de2 in this sense as "the receipt/capacity" (pp 274-75). The Wisdom tradition also uses de2 in the sense of an attainment able to protect the integrity of this

natural endowment. This attainment is termed "higher" (DDJ 38), "profound" (DDJ 14) and "great" (DDJ 21). Why designs for dominating natural holistic systems (harmonies) are thought to shorten longevity is not immediately clear. Qualities favoring longevity are said to be the supple, weak, and soft (DDJ 36, 76), while stiffness that makes for strength is characteristic of death. The Way of the Sages is a design for preserving the flexibility of response (DDJ 15). The free play involved in a flexible response capability lessens the precision of control, so that one draws closer to the pattern of the Way (which sustains without dominating—DDJ 34) by yielding a tight reign over things. Increasing the power to dominate would then have a negative impact on longevity, because the rigor required (to gain greater control) will distance the controller from the source of constancy—the flexible balancing of opposites in the Way's cyclical pattern of movement.

56. Profound Union

The anthropocentric idea that the constancy of the world is a product of superhuman design was pervasive in the ancient world, both East and West. The persistence of this idea more than three hundred years after the emergence of the modern scientific world-view is evidence of its tenacity. This conception of order in the universe was countered by the teachings of the Wisdom tradition transmitted in the *Dao De Jing*, which locate the source of constancy in the natural world in neither agency nor design. This naturalistic orientation makes it impossible for any human agency to assert a racial relation of descent, or one of favored dispensation, from the source of constancy.

57. Lesson in Governance I

Here examples of social conditions that obtain when the Way is abandoned are contrasted with the productive harmony that flourishes under wise governance. The world is "obtained" (DDJ 48) when constancy is protected by practices that preserve and assist self-ordering natural processes.

59. Political Ecology I
"Looking after nature" translates shi4 tian1. Literally it means "to serve Heaven." In the Wisdom tradition, however, Heaven is not a person to whom one can render service. Together with Earth, Heaven comprises the totality of nature. "To serve Heaven" is therefore a metaphor for looking after the natural processes of the world that arise without design and evolve stable order on their own.

61. Lesson in Governance V
Discussion of large-small state relations in this verse provides evidence that some of the thinking of the *Dao De Jing* antedates the Warring States period (480-221BCE). By the onset of this period the smaller feudal principalities of the Zhou clan confederacy had all but disappeared. In the Warring States period advice like that offered here becomes pointless.

62. The Way Is Honored by the World
This verse has several obscure historical references. "Storehouse" translates ao4 , the "sacred" southwest corner of the house where grain was kept. The "Son of Heaven" was the title assumed by the leader of the Zhou clan confederacy.

63. Wei Wu Wei I
The Quietist reading found in later Daoist texts mistakenly holds that the negation of all designing activity is the model found in the Wisdom tradition of the ancient sages (see the Comment to DDJ 80 and the Additional Comments for DDJ 3, 37, and 64). In the Wang Bi and other ancient texts the first stanza of

this verse has an additional line that is usually translated as "Respond to injury [resentment, grievance] with virtue's attainment" [bao4 yuan4 yi3 de2]. The line diverges from the focus on the small and appears to belong elsewhere. Duyvendak, citing the precedent of Ma Hsu-lun, transferred the line to DDJ 79, where it appears to fit in much better than here. I have followed this emendation.

64. Wei Wu Wei II

Just as in DDJ 14 where "Hold to the ancient Way" has "know the earliest beginnings" as its subordinate maxim, so in DDJ 63 and 64 the Wisdom strategy has awareness of incipient tendencies as a component of its method. The Wisdom of the ancient sages repeatedly stresses that nothing is more likely to defeat its design for social harmony and environmental stability than the failure of leaders to protect self-organizing activity from designing actions that "cut." Protective responses need to be made early when developing tendencies have not yet formed weighty trajectories.

The quietest view found in presentations of "Daoism," which takes the Wisdom method to be one of "non-action," is plainly inconsistent with the interventionist teaching of stanza one. But the final stanza, according to Lau, presents "two points of view" that "are not simply unconnected; they are inconsistent" (p. 167). The closing lines do say that the ancient sages both "assisted" the myriad things and "did not dare to act on them." But these statements are inconsistent only if one fails appreciate the difference between intervening holistically to protect constancy (sustainability) and intervening egoistically with designs to dominate and loot the natural order for private gain. The lines are inconsistent only in a mistaken interpretation of the ancient holistic wisdom method.

67. Wisdom's Three Treasures

Translations of the first line vary. The Mawangdui and Fu Yi texts do not have the word dao4 in the line, allowing the subject to be "I" instead of "dao:" "All under heaven say that I am great" (Mair translation). Another variation is possible because the language of the Classical texts uses the same character for "I" and "me." Thus, the Ch'u Ta-Kao translation has the line as "All the world says to me: 'Great as Tao is….'" Waley saw a pun on the word da4, used adverbially to mean "greatly" in the first line and as a predicate adjective meaning "great" in the second. The phrase "not much of anything" translates bu2 xiao4 and means literally "not resemble," but is known to have been a fixed expression meaning an unworthy, inferior, or below average condition or capacity.

68. Non-Contention

"Using the strength of others" [yong4 ren2 zhi1 li4] is not restricted to the martial arts, as the example we see employed in the next verse, DDJ 69, might suggest. It has an ecologically prior meaning in DDJ 6 in connection with "Heaven's root," which is said to be "continuously restored" and may therefore be used "without toil." The valuing of diversity (the myriad beings) through tolerance has the rationale, in the ancient sages' practice of the Way, of guarding (while using) the self-organizing processes of nature, so that "their strength" may both enrich the community and lighten the burden of human labor. It is by uniting human design activity with these non-designed, self-organizing processes so as to both "use" and protect their "constancy" that the world is said to be "obtained" (DDJ 48, 57). The ancient Wisdom design is a strategy in pursuit of the holistic aim of harmony by means of subordinating egoism and the acquisitive and accumulationist designs of desire. In the closing line this aim is expressed by the phrase pei4 tian1, translated variously as "matching," "pairing" or "being in harmony" with Heaven (the natural world). Pei4 tian1 requires the subordination of the ego, because the world's primary natural production is not governed by ego-driven designs. To say the Way is "constantly without a name" (DDJ 32) means no ego is involved in its functioning. Thus anonymity prevails, and the ancient sages teach this anonymity with their maxim "To make a contribution and then retire—this is the Way of Heaven" (DDJ 9).

70. Wisdom and Ignorance

The "lineage" of the speaker's words is the enlightened understanding transmitted by the ancient sages, who taught that the source of constancy in the universe is not, as commonly thought, the power to dominate and control, but is instead nature's capacity derived from its "unity" with the Great Way to sustain the continuity of Being. The "sovereign" of the speaker's teaching, therefore, is the Great Way itself. If the verse is viewed in relation to the preceding sequence (DDJ 59-69), in which the teachings are directed primarily to the heads of states, then it appears the opening line relates to the failure of political leaders to understand and put into practice the Wisdom of the Way.

71. A Disease of Ignorance

The idea that an ignorance of understanding (holistic wisdom) is a "sickness" merits further comment because it resonates with what has been said in earlier verses about the disordering effects of excess on personality. In DDJ 3 the equilibrium condition that equates with health and well-being was portrayed as one of sufficiency, that is, a condition in which there is neither deficiency nor excess. Because opposites arise together (DDJ 2), deficiency must therefore be seen as "the other side of excess." The recorded sayings transmitted in the *Dao De Jing* deal frequently with the debilitating opposition of excess and deficiency on the one hand, and with the Wisdom tradition's healing corrective of a return to sufficiency on the other. In the case of those in the hierarchy of social and political power the "disease" (failing or deficiency) implied by their ignorance of what is easy to understand must be linked, via the polarity of opposites "that arise together," to their excesses. It is therefore appropriate that the chapters immediately following DDJ 70 and 71 address the abusive excesses of the ruling elites (DDJ 72, 74 and 75). Placed in the era of the decline of the Zhou clan confederacy and the consanguineal state that organized its way of life, these actions suggest the addition of the underlying anxiety disorder that Diamond identified among non-laboring elites as stemming from "their dissociated dependence on the work of others" (p. 15), which in the verses cited above is the likely motivating factor behind their invasive security measures.

77. The Way of Heaven

The analogy of the bow is partial and limited by the fact that in nature there is no bowman or archer adjusting the tension in the bowstring. This functioning of the Way of Heaven (the recovery of sufficiency in place of the extremes of excess and want) is accomplished spontaneously and without any action of design. To bring the Way of Heaven into the human world of conscious design therefore requires a holistic counter-design to that of the particularistic ego-driven Way of Men. This is supplied by the Wisdom tradition, whose sages transcend the particularistic bias of the ego for enhancement and special benefits by following the Way of Heaven. They are therefore said *"not to hoard"* (DDJ 81). Commentators like Duyvendak, who follow Ma Hsu-lun, transfer this line from DDJ 81 to this verse where it supplies the needed counterpoint to the Way of Men. To follow Heaven is to integrate the part with the whole by subordinating the particularizing interests of ego designs to the non-designed self-balancing rhythms of nature, in order to make use of the strength and resiliency of its ecologies while at the same time guarding and preserving them. This holistic design answers the question that opens the third stanza. Followers of the Wisdom tradition do not hoard because their ultimate design is not to amass benefits, but to see that all benefits are "returned" rather than hoarded, that the flow of natural abundance is not blocked, and the equilibrium of sufficiency is not ruined by possessive, accumulationist designs. Their counter-design, therefore, is *to care for the world*, meaning the whole of life and the natural processes on which life depends.

78. Lesson in Governance VII
Concerning the second stanza, Duyvendak notes that the "dirt" refers to "the clod of earth taken from the Altar of Soil and Grain of the king, which was presented to a feudal lord as a token of his investiture, so as to erect with it an Altar of Soil and Grain in his own fief" (p. 159).

79. Reconciliation
The line "By responding to it with [wisdom's] attainment." was transferred here from DDJ 63, where it appears out of place. This follows the suggestion of Duyvendak, who cites the precedent of Ma Hsu-lun and Kao Heng (p. 160).

80. A Vision of Permaculture
"Knotted cords" likely refers to a type of record-keeping in a culture without writing. This verse is commonly given a political interventionist reading by interpreting the word shi3 to mean "cause to," or "make," rather than treating it as a function word meaning "if." Both meanings are possible. The former reading is found, for example, in Lau, whose translation was used by Schwartz in chapter 6 of his *The World of Thought in Ancient China*. Schwartz's comment is that the Taoist ruler "sees to it (lit.

"causes" *shih*) that [the technology available] is rejected" (p. 212). So influential has been the interventionist reading that even translators who begin by treating shi3 as meaning "supposing" (Ch'u Ta-kao) or "imagine" (Red Pine), resort to reading it in the traditional way. The suppositional reading given here explores the way the verse can be understood when shi3 is translated consistently as indicating hypothetical discourse. Ecologically sustainable communities were originally self-organizing, as they had to have been for generations before the emergence of political and administrative elites and the vertical civilizations founded by them. The closing lines about inhabitants in neighboring small states not traveling back and forth draws out what it means to live in self-sufficient sustainable communities. Since there is little need for or interest in trade and commerce, the principle motive for "comings and goings" is diminished.

81. The Way of the Sages

Sages do not hoard because they emulate Heaven (Nature) which does not hoard. Hoarding is absent in Nature because accumulations beyond sufficiency are energy vectors that cannot be sustained. The opening lines of the 2nd stanza are paradoxical unless it is understood that mutualism in society is the design correlate of the "sharing" that takes place without design in nature, where sufficiency is the basis of self-stabilizing order. The apparent paradox of "bettering one's own store" by supporting others dissolves when it is seen that "store" [duo1], in the sense of having something in abundance, a "big store," (Karlgren, p. 289), means the commons that is drawn upon in time of need. It is interesting to note that, whether by accident or design, the ecological teaching of the *Dao De Jing* forms the bookends of the standard text, which opens with the "Constant Way" (chang2 dao4) and closes with the "Way of the Sages" (sheng4 ren2 zhi1 dao4) that emulates it. The final line says that the sages "act" (wei2), which contradicts the traditional "Taoist" view that the "Way of the Sages" is *not to act*. Schwartz saw this as "a basic inconsistency," (*ibid.*), but what it actually shows is the inaccuracy and incoherence of the "Taoist" interpretation.

SELECTED BIBLIOGRAPHY

Translations and Commentaries:

Ames, Roger T. and Hall, David L.: *Daodejing, A Philosophical Translation* (Introductory essay, Chinese text, extensive commentary and notes). New York: Ballantine Books, 2003.

Blakney, R. B.: *The Way of Life, Lao Tzu, A New Translation of the Tao Te Ching* (Verse translation and paraphrases). New York: The New American Library of World Literature, 1955.

Chan, Wing-Tsit: *The Way of Lao Tzu (Tao Te Ching).* (Introductory essay, translation, commentary and notes; extensive bibliography of works in Chinese, Japanese and English). New Jersey: Prentice Hall, 1963.

Chang, Chung-yuan: *Tao: A New Way of Thinking.* (Introductory essay, translation, and commentary). New York: Harper & Row Publishers, 1975.

Chen, Ellen M.: *The Tao Te Ching, A New Translation with Commentary* (Introductory essay, translation and commentary). New York; Paragon House, 1989.

Ch'u, Ta-Kao: *Tao Te Ching* (Preface, translation and notes). London: George Allen & Unwin, 1959.

Duyvendak, J.J.L.: *Tao Te Ching, The Book of the Way and Its Virtue* (Introductory essay, translation and commentary). London: John Murray, 1954.

Erkes, Eduard: *Ho-Shang-Kung's Commentary on Lao-Tse.* (Translation of Ho-Shang-Kung text and commentary). Ascona, Switzerland: Artibus Asiae Publishers, 1950.

Ivanhoe, Philip J.: *The Daodejing of Laozi* (Introductory essay, translation and notes). New York: Seven Bridges Press, 2002.

Hendricks, Robert G.: *Lao Tzu Te-Tao Ching* (Introductory essay, translation of Mawangdui manuscripts, Chinese texts with notes). New York: Random House, 1989.

................: *Lao Tzu's Tao Te Ching* (Translation of the Guodian "Bamboo Slip Laozi," with Introductory essay, notes and appendices). New York: Columbia University Press, 2000.

Lau, D. C.: *Lao Tzu Tao Te Ching* (Introductory essay, translation , notes , two appended essays and glossary). New York: Penguin Books, 1963.

Lin, Paul J/Wang Bi.: *A Translation of Lao Tzu's Tao Te Ching and Wang Pi's Commentary.* Ann Arbor: The University of Michigan Monographs in Chinese Studies, Volume 30, 1977.

Lin Yutang: *The Wisdom of Laotse* (Translation with selections from the *Zhuangzi* added as commentary). New York: Random House, Modern Library Edition, 1948.

Lynn, Richard John/Wang Bi: *The Classic of the Way and Virtue* (Introductory essay, translation of the Wang Bi text and commentary with notes by Lynn). New York: Columbia University Press, 1999.

Mair, Victor: *Tao Te Ching, The Classic Book of Integrity and the Way* (Translation of the Mawangdui manuscripts with commentary and Afterword essay). New York: Bantam Doubleday Dell Publishing Group, 1990.

Red Pine: *Lao-Tzu's Taoteching* (Translation primarily of the Mawangdui texts, with selections from Chinese commentaries "of the past 2000 years"). San Francisco: Mercury House, 1996.

Roberts, Moss: *Dao De Jing, The Book of the Way* (Introductory essay, translation, commentary and notes). Berkeley: University of California Press, 2001.

Star, Jonathan: *Tao Te Ching, The Definitive Edition* (Translation, Wang Bi text in Chinese with Wade-Giles and Pinyin romanizations, Chinese-English concordance). New York: Tarcher/Putnam, 2001.

Waley, Arthur: *The Way and Its Power, A Study of the Tao Te Ching and Its Place in Chinese Thought* (Introductory essay, translation, commentary and notes). New York; The MacMillan Company, 1934.

Wilhelm, Richard: *Tao Te Ching, The Book Meaning and Life* (Introductory essay, English translation of German edition by H. G. Ostwald, commentary and notes). London: Routledge & Kegan Paul Inc, 1985.

Other Works:

Brooks, E. Bruce and Brooks. A. Taeko: *The Original Analects, Sayings of Confucius and His Successors*. New York: Columbia University Press, 1998.

Callicott, J. Baird: *Earth's Insights: A Multicultural Survey of Ecological Ethics from the Mediterranean Basin to the Australian Outback* (Berkeley: University of California Press, 1994.

Chan, Wing-Tsit: *A Sourcebook in Chinese Philosophy*. Princeton: Princeton University Press, 1963.

Clark, J. J.: *The Dao of the West: Western Transformations of Taoist Thought*. New York: Routledge, 2000.

Clastres, Pierre: *Society Against the State*. New York: Urzone, Inc. Zone Books, 1994. Originally published as *La Societe contre l'etat*, Paris: Editions de Minuit, 1974.

Cannon, Walter: *The Wisdom of the Body*. New York: W. W. Norton & Company, Inc., 1963. First published, 1932.

Diamond, Stanley: *In Search of the Primitive*. New Brunswick: Transaction Publishers, 1974

Dobson, W. A. C. H.: *Mencius*. Toronto: University of Toronto Press, 1963.

Ebehard, Wolfram: *A History of China*. Berkeley: University of California Press, 1977; originally published 1948; English translation by E. W. Dickes

Elias, Norbert: *The Court Society*. Oxford: Basil Blackwell, 1983.

Ereira, Alan: *The Elder Brothers, A Lost South American People and Their Message about the Fate of the Earth*. New York: Alfred A. Knopf, 1992.

Fung, Yu-lan: *Chuang-Tzu, A New Selected Translation with an Exposition of the Philosophy of Kuo Hsiang* (Bejing: Foreign Languages Press, 1989.

-----------------: *A Short History of Chinese Philosophy*. New York: The Free Press, 1976.

Gaster, Theodor H.: *Thespis: Ritual, Myth, and Drama in the Ancient Near East*. New York: W.W .Norton & Company, Inc., 1977.

Granet, Marcel: *Chinese Civilization*. Cleveland: The World Publishing Company, Meridian Books, 1958.

Graham, A. C.: *Disputers of the Tao, Philosophical Argument in Ancient China*. La Salle, IL: Open Court Publishing Company, 1989.

Henderson, John B.: *The Development and Decline of Chinese Cosmology*. New York: Columbia University Press, 1984.

Hsu, Cho-yun: *Ancient China in Transition. An Analysis of Social Mobility, 722-222 B.C.* Stanford. CA: Stanford University Press, 1965.

Kapchuck, Ted J.: *The Web That Has No Weaver*. Chicago: NTC/Contemporary Publishing Group, Inc., 2000.

Karlgren, Bernhard: *Analytic Dictionary of Chinese and Sino-Japanese.* New York: Dover Publications, Inc., 1974; original French edition: Librairie Orientalieste Paul Geuthner, 1923.

----------------------: *Sound & Symbol in Chinese.* Toronto: Global Language Press, 2007.

Kaufmann, Stuart: *At Home in the Universe, The Search for the Laws of Self-Organization and Complexity.* New York: Oxford University Press, 1995.

Kohn, Livia and LaFargue, Michael: *Lao Tzu and the Tao-Te-Ching.* Albany: State University of New York, 1998.

Kropotkin, Petr: *The State, Its Historic Role.* London: Freedom Press, 1969. First publication in France as *L'Etat—son role historique*, 1897.

Krader, Lawrence: *Formation of the State.* Englewood Cliffs, NJ: Prentice Hall, Inc. 1968.

Legge, James: *The Texts of Taoism*, Vols. I and II. New York; Dover Publications, Inc., 1962. Original publication : Oxford University Press, 1891.

Mair, Victor H.: *Wandering on the Way: Early Taoist Tales and Parables of Chuang Tzu.* Honolulu: University of Hawai'i Press, 1994.

Mote, F. W.: *Intellectual Foundations of China.* New York: Afred A. Knopf, 1971.

Odum, Eugene P.: *Fundamentals of Ecology*. Philadelphia: Saunders College Publishing/Hold, Rinehart and Winston, 3rd Edition, 1971.

Radin, Paul: *The World of Primitive Man*. New York: Henry Schuman, Inc. 1953.

Sahlins, Marshall: *Stone Age Economics*. New York: Aldine de Gruyter, 1972.

Schwartz, Benjamin I.: *The World of Thought in Ancient China*. Cambridge, MA: Harvard University Press, 1985.

Schuessler, Axel: *ABC Etymological Dictionary of Old Chinese*. Honolulu: University of Hawai'i Press, 2007.

Shakespeare, William: *The Tempest*. Hollywood, FL: Simon and Brown, 2011.

Turner, Scott: *The Tinkerer's Accomplice, How Design emerges from Life Itself*. Cambridge: Harvard University Press, 2007.

Van Der Ryn, Sim and Cowen, Stuart: *Ecological Design*. Washington, D.C.: Island Press, 1996.

Vagts, Alfred: *A History of Militarism, Civilian and Military*. New York: Simon & Schuster, 1981.

Wagner, Rudolf G.: *The Craft of A Chinese Commentator, Wang Bi on the Laozi*. Albany: State University of New York Press, 2000.

Waters, Frank: *Book of the Hopi*. New York: Viking Penguin, Inc., 1963.

Wieger, L., S.J.: *Chinese Characters, their Origin, Etymology, History, Classification and Signification*. New York: Dover Publications, 1965; original French edition, 1915.

Wenke, Robert J.: *Patterns in Prehistory, Humankind's First Three Million Years*. New York: Oxford University Press, 1984.

Wolf, Eric R.: *Europe and the People without History*. Berkeley: University of California Press, 1984.

Online Resources

Laozi Daodejing Siegelschrift (www.alice-dsl.net): Complete Sealscript and Full Form Characters of the Wang Bi text with pinyin romanization, dictionary meanings in English, German and French, and a concordance in Chinese.

Made in the USA
Las Vegas, NV
03 June 2022

49732540R00095